FAST SP.

WITH
Elisabeth Smith

FAST
SPANISH

HODDER
EDUCATION
AN HACHETTE UK COMPANY

For UK order enquiries: please contact
Bookpoint Ltd, 130 Milton Park, Abingdon, Oxon OX14 4SB.
Telephone: +44 (0) 1235 827720. Fax: +44 (0) 1235 400454.
Lines are open 09.00–17.00, Monday to Saturday, with a 24-hour
message answering service. Details about our titles and how to
order are available at www.teachyourself.com

For USA order enquiries: please contact McGraw-Hill Customer
Services, PO Box 545, Blacklick, OH 43004-0545, USA.
Telephone: 1-800-722-4726. Fax: 1-614-755-5645.

For Canada order enquiries: please contact McGraw-Hill
Ryerson Ltd, 300 Water St, Whitby, Ontario L1N 9B6, Canada.
Telephone: 905 430 5000. Fax: 905 430 5020.

Long renowned as the authoritative source for self-guided learning –
with more than 50 million copies sold worldwide – the **teach yourself**
series includes over 500 titles in the fields of languages, crafts,
hobbies, business, computing and education.

British Library Cataloguing in Publication Data: a catalogue record
for this title is available from the British Library.

Library of Congress Catalog Card Number: on file.

First published in UK 1998 as *Teach Yourself Instant Spanish*
by Hodder Education, part of Hachette UK, 338 Euston Road,
London NW1 3BH.

First published in US 1998 as *Teach Yourself Instant Spanish* by
The McGraw-Hill Companies, Inc.

This edition published 2011.

The **teach yourself** name is a registered trade mark of
Hodder Headline.

Typeset by MPS Limited, a Macmillan Company.

Printed in Great Britain for Hodder Education, a Hachette UK
Company, 338 Euston Road, London NW1 3BH, by CPI Cox &
Wyman, Reading, Berkshire RG1 8EX.

The publisher has used its best endeavours to ensure that the
URLs for external websites referred to in this book are correct and
active at the time of going to press. However, the publisher and
the author have no responsibility for the websites and can make
no guarantee that a site will remain live or that the content will
remain relevant, decent or appropriate.

Hachette UK's policy is to use papers that are natural, renewable
and recyclable products and made from wood grown in sustainable
forests. The logging and manufacturing processes are expected to
conform to the environmental regulations of the country of origin.

Impression number   10 9 8 7 6 5 4 3 2 1

Year   2014 2013 2012 2011

Contents

Read this first

If, like me, you usually skip introductions, don't. Read on. You need to know how **Fast Spanish with Elisabeth Smith** works and why. You'll want to know how you are going to speak Spanish in just six weeks.

When I decided to write this series I first called it *Barebones*, because that's what you want: no frills, no fuss, just the bare bones and go. So in **Fast Spanish with Elisabeth Smith** you'll find:

- Only 393 words to say, well … nearly everything.
- No tricky grammar – just some useful tips.
- No time wasters such as *the pen of my aunt…*
- No phrase book phrases for when you take Flamenco lessons in Bilbao.
- No need to be perfect. Mistakes won't spoil your success.

I've put some 30 years of teaching experience into this course. I know how people learn. I also know how long they are motivated by a new project before the boredom sets in (a few weeks). And I am well aware how little time they can spare to study each day (about ½ hour). That's why you'll complete **Fast Spanish with Elisabeth Smith** in six weeks and get away with 35 minutes a day.

Of course there is some learning to do, but I have tried to make it as much fun as possible. You'll meet Tom and Kate Walker on holiday in Spain. They do the kind of things you need to know about: shopping, eating out and getting about. They chat to the locals, ask a lot of questions and even understand the answers – most of the time. As you will note, Tom and Kate speak Spanish all the time, even to each other. What paragons of virtue!

To get the most out of this course, there are only three things you really should do:

- Follow the **Day-by-day guide** as suggested. Please don't skip bits and short-change your success. Everything is there for a reason.

- If you are a complete beginner and have only bought the book, treat yourself to the recording as well. It will help you to speak faster and with confidence.
- Don't skip the next page (**How this book works**). It's essential for your success.

When you have filled in your **Certificate** at the end of the book and can speak **Fast Spanish with Elisabeth Smith**, I would like to hear from you. Why not visit my website www.elisabeth-smith.co.uk, e-mail me at elisabeth.smith@hodder.co.uk, or write to me care of Hodder Education, 338 Euston Road, London, NW1 3BH?

And please join me on:

Facebook at www.facebook.com/elisabethsmithlanguages

Twitter at www.twitter.com/LanguagesESmith

Elizabeth Smith

How this book works

Fast Spanish with Elisabeth Smith has been structured for your rapid success. This is how it works:

Day-by-day guide Stick to it. If you miss a day, add one.

Dialogues Follow Tom and Kate through Spain. The English of Weeks 1–3 is in 'Spanish-speak' to get you tuned in. 'Spanish-speak' is English imitating the expressions and word order of Spanish: *We have a house big without telephone.* You'll soon get a feel for the language.

New words Don't fight them, don't skip them – learn them! The **Flash cards** and the recording will help you. Get your friends or family to test you. Or take the **Flash cards** with you when you are out and about.

Good news grammar After you read it you can forget half and still succeed. That's why it's good news.

Flash words and flash sentences Read about these building blocks in the **Flash card section**. Then use them! They'll reduce learning time by 50%.

Learn by heart Obligatory! Memorizing puts you on the fast track to speaking in full sentences. When you know all six pieces you'll be able to speak in Spanish for six minutes without drawing breath.

Let's speak Spanish You will be doing the talking – in Spanish.

Let's speak more Spanish – fast and fluently Optional extras for more speaking practice without pausing and stumbling.

Spot the keys Listen to rapid Spanish and make sense of it. Find the key words among a seemingly unintelligible string of sentences and get the gist of what's being said – an essential skill.

Say it simply Learn how to use Simple Spanish to say what you want to say. Don't be shy.

Test your progress Mark your own test and be amazed by the result.

Answers This is where you'll find the answers to the exercises.

🔊 This icon asks you to switch on the recording.

Pronunciation If you don't know about it and don't have the recording go straight to Week 1 **Pronunciation**. You need to know about pronunciation before you can start Week 1.

Progress chart Enter your score each week and monitor your progress. Are you going for very good or outstanding?

Dictionary Forgotten one of the new words? Look it up in the dictionary.

Certificate It's on the last page. In six weeks it will have your name on it.

Progress chart

At the end of each week record your test score on the progress chart below.

At the end of the course throw out your worst result – anybody can have a bad week – and add up your five best weekly scores. Divide the total by five to get your average score and overall course result. Write your result – outstanding, excellent, very good or good – on your **Certificate** at the end of the book.

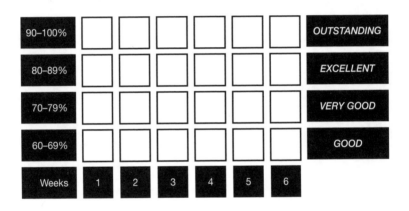

Total of five best weeks =

divided by five =

Your final result _____%

Week 1

Day-by-day guide

Invest 35 minutes a day – or a little more if you can.

Day zero

- Open the book and read **Read this first**.
- Now read **How this book works**.

Day one

- Read **In the aeroplane**.
- Listen to/Read **En el avión**.
- Listen to/Read the **New words**, then learn some of them.

Day two

- Repeat **En el avión** and the **New words**.
- Listen to/Read **Pronunciation**.
- Learn more **New words**.
- Use the **Flash words** to help you.

Day three

- Learn all the **New words** until you know them well.
- Read and learn the **Good news grammar**.

Day four

- Cut out and learn the ten **Flash sentences**.
- Listen to/Read **Learn by heart**.

Day five

- Listen to/Read **Let's speak Spanish**.
- Revise! Tomorrow you'll be testing your progress.

Day six

- Listen to/Read **Let's speak more Spanish** (optional).
- Listen to/Read **Let's speak Spanish – fast and fluently** (optional).
- Translate **Test your progress**.

Day seven – This is your day off.

In the aeroplane

Tom and Kate Walker are off to Spain. They board a plane to Malaga via Barcelona and squeeze past a fellow passenger sitting in their now.

Don't forget that the English of Weeks 1–3 is in 'Spanish-speak' to help you get used to the way the language works.

Tom Excuse me, we have the seats four a and four b.

Pedro Ah, yes, a moment please.

Tom Hello, how are you? We are Tom and Kate Walker.

Pedro Good morning, I call myself (My name is) Iglesias.

Tom Julio Iglesias?

Pedro No, come off it! My name is Pedro Iglesias.

Tom We are going to Malaga. And you?

Pedro No, I am going to Barcelona but I am from Seville.

Tom Seville? I was in Seville in May – for my company.

Pedro In what do you work?

Tom I work with computers.

Pedro And you, Mrs Walker?

Kate Well… I have worked in Mobil three years. Now I work in Rover.

Pedro Are you from London?

Kate No, we are from Manchester. We have been one year in New York and two years in London. Now we work in Birmingham.

Pedro I have worked four years in Seat but now I work in the Bank of Spain.

Tom And how is the work in the bank? Is it good?

Pedro The work is boring but the pay is better. I have a house big, a Mercedes and four children. My wife is American from Los Angeles and she has a girlfriend in Dallas. She talks always with her on the telephone and goes always to Los Angeles. It costs a lot of money.

Kate And are you now also on holiday?

Pedro No, unfortunately not. We have always the holidays in September. We are going to Mallorca but without the children. We have a house in Palma without telephone, and we go there without mobile!

En el avión

🔊 CD1, tr 2

Tom and Kate Walker are off to Spain. They board a plane to Malaga via Barcelona and squeeze past a fellow passenger sitting in their now.

Tom Perdone, tenemos los asientos cuatro a y cuatro b.

Pedro ¡Ah! sí, un momento por favor.

Tom Hola, ¿Qué tal? Somos Tom y Kate Walker.

Pedro Buenos días. Me llamo Iglesias.

Tom ¿Julio Iglesias?

Pedro No, ¡qué va! Me llamo Pedro Iglesias.

Tom Nosotros vamos a Málaga. ¿Y usted?

Pedro No, yo voy a Barcelona pero soy de Sevilla.

Tom ¿Sevilla? He estado en Sevilla en mayo – para mi empresa.

Pedro ¿En qué trabaja?

Tom Trabajo con ordenadores.

Pedro ¿Y usted, Señora Walker?

Kate Pues… yo he trabajado en Mobil tres años. Ahora trabajo en Rover.

Pedro ¿Es de Londres?

Kate No, somos de Manchester. Hemos estado un año en Nueva York y dos años en Londres. Ahora trabajamos en Birmingham.

Pedro Yo he trabajado cuatro años en Seat pero ahora trabajo en el Banco de España.

Tom ¿Y qué tal el trabajo en el banco? ¿Es bueno?

Pedro El trabajo es aburrido pero el sueldo es mejor. Tengo una casa grande, un Mercedes y cuatro niños. Mi mujer es americana, de Los Ángeles, y tiene una amiga en Dallas. Habla siempre con ella por teléfono y va siempre a Los Ángeles. Cuesta mucho dinero.

Kate ¿Y está ahora también de vacaciones?

Pedro No, desgraciadamente no. Tenemos siempre las vacaciones en septiembre. Vamos a Mallorca, pero sin los niños. Tenemos una casa en Palma sin teléfono, ¡y vamos allí sin móvil!

3

New words

🔊 CD1, tr 3

Learning words the traditional way can be boring. If you enjoy the **Flash cards** why not make your own for the rest of the words. Always say the words out loud.

en in/on
el, la, los, las the
el avión the aeroplane
perdón excuse me
tenemos we have
los asientos the seats
cuatro four
a, b pronounced 'uh', 'bay'
y and
sí yes
un momento a moment
por favor please
hola hello
¿qué tal? how are you, how is…?
somos we are
buenos días good day, good morning
me llamo my name is…
no no, not
¡qué va! come off it!
nosotros we
vamos we go, we are going, let's go!
a/al to, to the
usted/ustedes you (one person)/ you (more than one person)
yo I
voy I go, I am going
pero but
soy I am
de/del from, of/from, of the
he estado I have been, I was
mayo May
para for
mi my

la empresa the company
qué what
trabaja he/she/it works, you work
trabajo I work, also: (the) work
con with
ordenador/es computer/s
señora Mrs, woman
pues… well…, well then
he trabajado I have worked
tres three
el año, los años the year, the years
ahora now
es you are, he/she/it is
hemos estado we have been, we were
un, una a, one
dos two
trabajamos we work
el Banco de España the Bank of Spain
bueno/a good
aburrido/a boring
el sueldo the pay, salary
mejor better
tengo I have
una casa/en casa a house/ at home
grande big
los niños the children
la mujer the woman, wife
Americana American
tiene he/she/it has, you have
una amiga a girlfriend
habla he/she/it speaks, you speak

siempre always
ella she, her
por teléfono on the telephone
va he/she/it goes, you go
cuesta/cuestan it costs/they cost
mucho/a much, a lot
el dinero the money
está he/she/it is, you are

también also
de vacaciones on holiday(s)
desgraciadamente unfortunately
septiembre September
sin without
el (teléfono) móvil the mobile (phone)
allí there

> TOTAL NEW WORDS: 78
> … 315 words to go

Some easy extras

Los meses *(the months)*

enero	abril	julio	octubre
febrero	mayo	agosto	noviembre
marzo	junio	septiembre	diciembre

Números *(numbers)*

cero, uno, dos, tres, cuatro, cinco, seis, siete, ocho, nueve, diez

0	1	2	3	4	5	6	7	8	9	10

More greetings

buenas tardes	*good afternoon*	**buenas noches**	*good night*
hasta luego	*bye, until later*	**adiós**	*goodbye, for longer absence*

Pronunciation

🔊 CD1, tr 4

The Spanish language is beautiful, so drop all inhibitions and try to speak Spanish – not English with the words changed.

If Spanish pronunciation is new to you, please buy the recording. But if you are good at languages, or would like a refresher, here are the rules:

1 Vowels

The word in brackets gives you an example of the sound. Say the sound out loud and then the Spanish examples out loud.

When you listen to Spanish being spoken some of the sounds seem to vary a little from the example you find in the brackets. Don't worry about it. When you try to copy the sounds, near enough is good enough.

a	(*lamp*)	c**a**sa, M**á**laga, dí**a**s, v**a**mos
e	(*best*)	**e**s, p**e**ro, bu**e**no, tel**é**fono
i	(*seat*)	s**í**, s**i**n, m**i**, d**í**as, as**i**entos
o	(*not*)	n**o**, c**o**n, s**o**m**o**s, m**o**ment**o**
u	(*June*)	**u**n, **u**sted, c**u**esta, m**u**cho

All vowels are pronounced separately:

b**u**–**e**–no, as**i**–en–tos, e–**u**-ro.

2 Consonants

h	(-)	The 'h' is silent and is not pronounced at all: **h**ola, **h**e, **h**emos, **h**abla, a**h**ora.
j	(lo**ch**)	Like the guttural sound in the Scottish word loch: **j**ulio, traba**j**o, mu**j**er.
ll	(*yes/mi*lli*on*)	It is a bit of each. When you say **me llamo** the **ll** sounds like a **y**, but when you say **calle** it's more like the **lyer** sound in *million*. If your tongue gives up, stay with the **y**. Say: a**ll**í, Sevi**ll**a.
ñ	(*cany*on)	Watch out when you see the little wriggle on the top of the **n**: a**ñ**o, ni**ñ**o (say anyo, ninyo) Espa**ñ**a.
qu	(**k**ettle)	**qu**é, **qu**ince (15), **qu**inientos (500)

r	Give this a vigorous, throaty roll:	abu**rrrr**ido.
z	(**th**is)	The moment you spot a **z**, it's a lisp: **cerveza** (*beer*), **izquierda** (*left*), **trozo** (*piece*).
c + **e** or **i**	(**th**eft)	This is a lisp: **Barcelona**, **cinco**, **desgraciadamente**.
c + any other letter	(**c**ut, **c**lear)	Just like in English: **casa**, **con**, **cuatro**, **claro**.
g + **e** or **i**	(lo**ch**)	It's back to the throaty **ch** of *loch!* Luckily there are only two 'fast' words with **ge** or **gi**: **gente** and **colegio**.
g + any other letter	(**g**o, **g**ust)	Just like in English: **grande**, **golf**, **guapo**.

3 The stress

You stress the second syllable from the end: **mo-*men*-to, tra-*ba*-jo, va-mos, te-*ne*-mos, or-de-na-*do*-res**. But when there's a written accent, stress that part: **a-*llí*, te-*lé*-fo-no**.

Congratulations for having worked through the rules of pronunciation!

Good news grammar

🔊 CD1, tr 5

This is the **Good news** part of each lesson. Remember, I promised: no confusing grammar! Every week I explain just a few things and talk you through the differences between English and Spanish. This will help you to speak Spanish easily.

1 Names of things – nouns

There are two kinds of nouns in Spanish: masculine and feminine.

You can tell which is which by the word **el** or **la**, or **un** or **una** in front of the word. You can also tell by the ending of the noun.

Words ending in **-o** are masculine: **el dinero** or **un banco**.
Words ending in **-a** are feminine: **la casa** or **una amiga**.

The adjective describing a noun also ends in **-o** or **-a**. So *the good bank* becomes **el banco bueno**. *A good house* becomes **una casa buena**.

Unfortunately, not all nouns and adjectives behave so obediently. Some nouns end in any old letter: **la mujer** or **la televisión** (*the TV*), and some adjectives, like **grande**, do not change. And then there is **el día**, just to confuse you.

But these non-conformists are in the minority, so most of the time you can get it right … **el banco bueno … una amiga buena**.

When there is more than one thing (plural) **el** becomes **los**. All the rest just add an **s: los bancos buenos, las amigas buenas**.

Good news: If you get muddled and say **los casas buenos**, nobody is going to throw a fit. Everyone will understand you perfectly.

2 Doing things – verbs

This is a bit of bad news in Spanish, so brace yourself!

Unlike the English, the Spanish do not use *I*, *you*, *he*, *she*, *it*, *we*, or *they* to identify *who* is doing something unless they wish to clarify or stress it. So most of the time the only way you can tell *who is doing something* is by the *verb itself*.

Each person has his/her own form of verb ending, but sometimes an ending is shared. This could lead to some confusion, but amazingly it usually works out all right.

There are a handful of verbs which you'll need every day. Spend ten minutes on each. **Trabajar** belongs to the Good Verbs Group. These verbs all have the same endings. Know one – know them all.

	trabajar (to) work		**tener** (to) have	
(yo)	**trabajo**	*I work*	**tengo**	*I have*
(usted)	**trabaja**	*you work*	**tiene**	*you have*
(él)	**trabaja**	*he, it works*	**tiene**	*he, it has*
(ella)	**trabaja**	*she, it works*	**tiene**	*she, it has*
(nosotros)	**trabajamos**	*we work*	**tenemos**	*we have*
(ellos, ellas)	**trabajan**	*they work*	**tienen**	*they have*
(ustedes)	**trabajan**	*you work*	**tienen**	*you have*

(Usted) trabaja – (ustedes) trabajan: **trabaja** is used when talking to one person, **trabajan**, when talking to more than one. Spanish has two other words for you: **tú** and **vosotros**. These are informal and familiar and need extra endings. You don't need them for **Fast Spanish with Elisabeth Smith** – just use **usted** and **ustedes** or the verb form that goes with them. **¿Trabaja, Kate? ¿Trabajan, Tom y Kate?** Too much to take in? Will you remember all these endings? Don't worry! By Week 3 it will be a piece of cake!

3 Asking questions

Es bueno. *It is good*. **¿Es bueno?** *Is it good?* You simply use your voice to turn a statement into a question.

Learn by heart

🔊 CD1, tr 6

Don't be tempted to skip this exercise because it reminds you of school… If you want to speak, not stumble, saying a few lines by heart does the trick! Learn **Me llamo** by heart after you have filled in the gaps with your personal, or any, information.

Example   **Me llamo *Sarah Lawson*. Soy de *Newcastle*.**

When you know the lines by heart, go over them again until you can say them out loud fluently and fairly fast. Can you beat 40 seconds? Excellent! Give **Me llamo** a bit of life. You'll remember it better that way.

Me llamo…

Me llamo .... (*name*).

Soy de .... (*place*).

He estado en ....(*place*) en .... (*month*).

He trabajado en .... (*name of firm*) tres años.

Ahora trabajo en .... (*name of firm*).

Tengo una casa en .... (*place*) y cuesta mucho.

En agosto vamos a .... (*place*).

¿Qué tal Marbella en enero, bueno o aburrido?

Let's speak Spanish

I shall give you ten English sentences and you'll put them into Spanish. Always speak out loud. After each one check the answer overleaf or on the recording. Tick it if you got it right.

1 Hello, my name is Walker.
2 Are you from London?
3 Yes, I am from London.
4 We are going home. Bye!
5 I work with Pedro in Palma.
6 Do you have a Mercedes?
7 No, unfortunately not.
8 We have a house in Marbella.
9 How is the work, good?
10 Boring, but the pay is good.

Well, how many did you get right? If you are not happy, do them again.

Here are some questions in Spanish and you are going to answer in Spanish. Answer the first five with **sí**, and talk about yourself. In questions 16–20 I am talking to you and your friend. Say **sí** and *we*.

11 ¿Es de Bristol?
12 ¿Tiene una casa en Londres?
13 Pepe va a Granada. ¿Y usted?
14 ¿Tiene teléfono?
15 ¿Trabaja con ordenadores?
16 Vamos a casa. ¿Y ustedes?
17 Trabajamos en Los Ángeles. ¿Y ustedes?
18 Tenemos amigos en Málaga. ¿Y ustedes?
19 Vamos a Sevilla. ¿Y ustedes?
20 Tenemos un trabajo aburrido. ¿Y ustedes?

Answers

1 Hola, me llamo Walker.
2 Es de Londres?
3 Sí, soy de Londres.
4 Vamos a casa. ¡Hasta luego!
5 Trabajo con Pedro en Palma.
6 ¿Tiene un Mercedes?
7 No, desgraciadamente, no.
8 Tenemos una casa en Marbella.
9 ¿Qué tal el trabajo, bueno?
10 Aburrido, pero el sueldo es bueno.
11 Sí, soy de Bristol.
12 Sí, tengo una casa en Londres.
13 Sí, voy a Granada.
14 Sí, tengo teléfono.
15 Sí, trabajo con ordenadores.
16 Sí, vamos a casa.
17 Sí, trabajamos en Los Ángeles.
18 Sí, tenemos amigos en Málaga.
19 Sí, vamos a Sevilla.
20 Sí, tenemos un trabajo aburrido.

Well, what was your score? For 20/20 give yourself a pat on the back.

Let's speak more Spanish

Here are some optional exercises. They may stretch the 35 minutes a day by an extra 15 minutes. But the extra practice will be worth it.

And always remember: near enough is good enough!

In your own words

This exercise will teach you to express yourself freely. Use only the words you have learned so far.

Tell me in your own words that...

> *Example* **you are Peter Smith Soy Peter Smith.**

1 you originate from Manchester
2 you have an American friend
3 you are a workaholic... (you work much)
4 but you don't have a lot of cash
5 you have two children
6 the children are six and eight (have six and eight years)
7 unfortunately you work with a PC; it's boring
8 your wife works for a company in Bath
9 you own a property in Valencia
10 you have a holiday in April

Answers

1 Soy de Manchester.
2 Tengo un amigo americano/una amiga americana.
3 Trabajo mucho…
4 pero no tengo mucho dinero.
5 Tengo dos niños.
6 Los niños tienen seis y ocho años.
7 Desgraciadamente trabajo con un ordenador; es aburrido.
8 Mi mujer trabaja para una empresa en Bath.
9 Tengo una casa en Valencia.
10 Tengo las vacaciones en abril.

Let's speak Spanish – fast and fluently

🔊 CD1, tr 9

No more stuttering and stumbling! Get out the stopwatch and time yourself with this fluency practice.

Translate each section and check if it is correct, then cover up the answers and say the three or four sentences fast! Some of the English is in 'Spanish-speak' to help you.

Good evening. I am going to Madrid. You, too?
No, I work in Madrid – in a bank. Now I am going to Salamanca.
I have the holidays – without the computer.

Buenas noches. Voy a Madrid. ¿Usted también?
No, trabajo en Madrid – en un banco. Ahora voy a Salamanca.
Tengo las vacaciones – sin el ordenador.

How is Salamanca? Is it big?
It is not big, but it is not boring.
And it does not cost a lot.
I have a girlfriend, Carmen.

¿Qué tal Salamanca? ¿Es grande?
No, no es grande, pero no es aburrida.
Y no cuesta mucho.
Tengo una amiga, Carmen.

She has a house in Salamanca.
A hotel costs a lot of money.
Oh, excuse me. One moment, please, it is Carmen.
She is always speaking on the phone.
Bye!

Tiene una casa en Salamanca.
Un hotel cuesta mucho dinero.
Ah perdón, un momento, por favor, es Carmen.
Siempre habla por teléfono.
¡Hasta luego!

Now say all the sentences in Spanish without stopping and starting.

Test your progress

This is your only written exercise. You'll be amazed at how easy it is!
Translate the 20 sentences without looking at the previous pages. The
bits in brackets tell you how it is said in Spanish.

1 My name is Peter Smith.
2 Hello, we are Helen and Pepe.
3 I am from Toledo. And you?
4 María is a good friend.
5 I always go home in June.
6 We work in Alicante in August.
7 Do you always go to New York in March?
8 What work do you do? (In what do you work?) Do you work with
 computers?
9 She is in London with the children.
10 One moment, please. What is it? Does it cost a lot?
11 Does the house have a telephone? No, unfortunately not.
12 Good day. Are you (the) Mrs López from Madrid?
13 I work without pay at an American company.
14 Now I have a better job. I work for three big banks.
15 Paco! How are you? Are we going to Seville?
16 My wife also is American. She is from Boston.
17 We have good seats in the aeroplane.
18 Do I have a Mercedes? Come off it!
19 My girlfriend speaks Spanish (**español**), but not a lot.
20 I am going on holiday with Carmen. Unfortunately she is boring.

When you have finished look up the answers in the **Answers** section,
and mark your work. Then enter your result on the **Progress chart**
at the front of the book. If your score is higher than 80%, you'll have
done very well indeed!

Week 2

Day-by-day guide

35 minutes a day – but a little extra will step up your progress.

Day one
- Read **In (the) Sierra Nevada**.
- Listen to/Read **En Sierra Nevada**.
- Listen to/Read the **New words**. Learn 20 easy ones.

Day two
- Repeat **En Sierra Nevada** and the **New words**.
- Go over **Pronunciation**.
- Learn the harder **New words**.
- Use the **Flash words** to help you.

Day three
- Learn all the **New words** until you know them well.
- Read and learn the **Good news grammar**.

Day four
- Cut out and learn the **Flash sentences**.
- Listen to/Read **Learn by heart**.

Day five
- Listen to/Read **Let's speak Spanish**.
- Go over **No tengo mucho dinero, pero...**

Day six
- Listen to/Read **Let's speak more Spanish** (optional).
- Listen to/Read **Let's speak Spanish – fast and fluently** (optional).
- Translate **Test your progress**.

Day seven is a study-free day.

In (the) Sierra Nevada

Tom and Kate hire a car and drive to the Sierra Nevada. They book into a hotel and then look for somewhere to have a drink.

Kate	Good afternoon. Have you a room double for one night and not very expensive, please?
Hotelier	Yes, I have a room small with bathroom. But the shower is broken. My husband it can repair tomorrow.
Tom	Right, where is the room?
Hotelier	Here on the left. Not it is very big.
Kate	The room is a little small but nice. How much costs it?
Hotelier	Only €35 but we do not take credit cards. There is a big breakfast from eight to ten and half.
Kate	All right, we take the room. But can we take the breakfast at eight less quarter? We would like to go to Marbella tomorrow at eight and quarter.
Hotelier	Agreed.
Kate	Can I ask you where we can we take coffee? Is there near here a cafeteria… or a bar? Where are they?
Hotelier	It is very easy. There is a cafeteria at five minutes from here, at some 30 metres on the right and then straight ahead.

(In the cafeteria)

Waiter	What would you like to take, please?
Kate	We would like a coffee with milk and a tea, please.
Waiter	And something to eat? We have snacks, omelette, toast…
Tom	Right… two toasts, please.
Tom	The table is not clean.
Kate	Yes, but the cafeteria is not bad.
Tom	My tea is cold.
Kate	Yes, but the toilets are great.
Tom	The toast is bad.
Kate	Yes, but the waiter is very handsome.
Tom	I would like the bill, please.
Waiter	€9.10, please.

En Sierra Nevada

◀)) CD1, tr 10

Tom and Kate hire a car and drive to the Sierra Nevada. They book into a hotel and then look for somewhere to have a drink.

Kate　　Buenas tardes, ¿tiene usted una habitación doble para una noche y no muy cara, por favor?

Hotelier　Sí, tengo una habitación pequeña con cuarto de baño. Pero la ducha está rota. Mi marido la puede reparar mañana.

Tom　　Bueno, ¿dónde está la habitación?

Hotelier　Aquí, a la izquierda. No es muy grande.

Kate　　La habitación es un poco pequeña pero bonita. ¿Cuánto cuesta?

Hotelier　Sólo treinta y cinco euros, pero no tomamos tarjetas de crédito. Hay un desayuno de ocho a diez y media.

Kate　　Vale, tomamos la habitación. Pero, ¿podemos tomar el desayuno a las ocho menos cuarto? Quisiéramos ir a Marbella mañana a las ocho y cuarto.

Hotelier　De acuerdo.

Kate　　¿Puedo preguntarle dónde podemos tomar café? ¿Hay aquí cerca una cafetería… o un bar? ¿Dónde están?

Hotelier　Es muy fácil. Hay una cafetería a cinco minutos de aquí, a unos treinta metros a la derecha y luego todo recto.

(En la cafetería)

Waiter　¿Qué desean tomar, por favor?

Kate　　Quisiéramos un café con leche y un té, por favor.

Waiter　Y ¿algo para comer? Tenemos tapas, tortilla, tostadas…

Tom　　Bueno… dos tostadas por favor.

Tom　　La mesa no está limpia.

Kate　　Sí, pero la cafetería no es mala.

Tom　　Mi té está frío.

Kate　　Sí, pero los servicios son estupendos.

Tom　　La tostada está mala.

Kate　　Sí, pero el camarero es muy guapo.

Tom　　Quisiera la cuenta, por favor.

Waiter　Nueve euros y diez céntimos, por favor.

19

New words

🔊 CD1, tr 11

una habitación doble a double room
una noche a night
muy very
caro/a expensive
pequeño/a small
el cuarto de baño the bathroom
la ducha the shower
roto/a broken, broken down
el marido the husband
lo, la (by itself) it
puede he/she can, you can
reparar (to) repair
mañana tomorrow
bueno/a (by itself) all right, right
¿dónde? where?
aquí here
a la izquierda on the left
un poco a little
bonito/a pretty, lovely, nice
¿cuánto? how much…?
solo only
treinta y cinco 35
tomamos we take
las tarjetas de crédito the credit cards
el desayuno the breakfast
hay there is
medio half
vale all right, OK
podemos we can
tomar (to) take
menos less

cuarto quarter
quisiera/quisiéramos I/we would like (to)
ir (to) go
de acuerdo agreed, OK
puedo I can
preguntar to ask
¿puedo preguntarle? can I ask you?
café coffee
cerca near
una cafetería a café
o or
están they are, you are (plural)
fácil easy
minutos minutes
unos, unas some
treinta metros thirty metres
a la derecha on the right
luego then, later
todo recto straight ahead
¿qué desean? what do you want/wish?
la leche the milk
un té a tea
algo something
comer (to) eat
¿qué tienen ustedes? what do you have?
tapas Spanish snacks
una tortilla a Spanish omelette
tostadas toast
la mesa the table

limpio/a clean
frío/a cold
malo/a bad
los servicios the toilets
son are, they are

estupendo/a marvellous, great
el camarero the waiter
guapo/a good-looking
la cuenta the bill
el céntimo cent

> **TOTAL NEW WORDS: 70**
> ... only 245 words to go!

Good news grammar

◀» CD1, tr 12

1 *Ser* and *estar*: 'to be' and (not) 'to be'

Unless you are a genius you are bound to get these two mixed up at times. But with **Fast Spanish with Elisabeth Smith** everybody will still understand you perfectly. Here are the main differences between **ser** and **estar** which both mean *(to) be*.

You use **ser** when you talk about something which is a basic characteristic of somebody or something and which does not change.

> **Mi nombre *es* Paco.** *My name is Paco.* **Soy Paco.** *I am Paco.*
> **Somos ingleses.** *We are English.*

You also use **ser** for telling the time.

> **¿Qué hora *es*?** *What is the time?*
> **Son las tres.** *It is three (o'clock).* Literally: *They are the three.*

You use **estar** when you talk about something that is temporary, that can change.

> **Las mesas no *están* limpias.** *The tables are not clean.*
> **La ducha *está* rota.** *The shower is broken.*

You also use **estar** when someone or something is in a place, even if it is permanent.

> **Estamos en España.** *We are in Spain.*
> **Londres *está* en Inglaterra.** *London is in England.*
> **¿Dónde *está*?** *Where are you?* **Está aquí cerca.** *It is near here.*
> **Estoy en Barcelona.** *I am in Barcelona.*

And if you confuse them? Don't worry. It's not that serious.

Here is a combined verb box. Spend five minutes on it.

ser		estar
soy... Juan	*I am*	estoy... en Madrid
es	*you are*	está
es	*he/she/it is*	está
somos	*we are*	estamos
son	*they are*	están
son	*you are*	están

Remember, you and you: use **es** and **está** when you talk to one person. Use **son** and **están** when you talk to two people or more.

2 Saying 'not'

If you want to say in Spanish that you are not doing something, you just add **no**. But did you notice what happened to the **no** when Señora López said: *No es muy grande* and *No tomamos tarjetas?* The *not* moved in front of the verb. It does this all the time: *...**not** is very big, ...**not** we take credit cards*.

> **La mesa *no* está limpia**. *The table is not clean.*
> ***No* trabajo**. *I do not work.*

***No, no* trabajo**. Don't let this confuse you. The first **no** means *no*, the second one *not*.

3 *Hay:* there is/is there? – there are/are there?

You will use this a lot, especially when asking questions.

> ***¿Hay* un banco aquí cerca? *¿Hay* un bar? *¿Hay* servicios?**
> ***¿Hay* un camarero guapo? ¡Sí, *hay* dos!**

4 Telling the time

las siete menos cuarto	*quarter to seven*
las diez y cuarto	*quarter past ten*
las dos y media	*half past two*
la una y media	*half past one*

Learn by heart

◀) CD1, tr 13

Learn the six lines **No tengo mucho dinero, pero...** by heart.

When you know them try to say them fluently and fairly fast. How about 45 to 60 seconds?

Choose one of these to fill in the gaps: **mi marido**, **mi mujer**, **mi amigo** (boy/male friend), **mi amiga**.

No tengo mucho dinero, pero...

No tengo mucho dinero pero quisiera ir de vacaciones en julio.

Quisiera ir a la Costa del Sol con... .

Podemos ir a Marbella en el Rover.

No cuesta mucho y la Costa es muy bonita.

¿Podemos ir? ¡No!

Hay siempre mucho trabajo en la empresa y... ¡el Rover está roto!

Once again, bring this piece to life when you know it by heart by giving it lots of expression. Bits of it will come in handy later!

Let's speak Spanish

🔊 CD1, tr 14

Now let's practise what you have learned. Below I give you ten English sentences and you say them in Spanish – out loud. If you have the recording, listen to check the answers. Tick each sentence if you got it right. Unless you get nine correct, do the exercise again.

1 Do you have a room?
2 It is a little big.
3 At what time is the breakfast?
4 The computers are expensive.
5 We would like to eat something.
6 How much is (costs) the tea?
7 Where is the café? On the right?
8 We are going to Málaga at two.
9 Excuse me, the bill, please.
10 Is there a bank near here?

Now answer the questions on the left with **sí** and speak about yourself, and those on the right with **no** and say *we*.

11 ¿Tiene una tarjeta Visa?
12 ¿Hay un bar aquí?
13 ¿Es una cuenta muy grande?
14 ¿Están de vacaciones?
15 ¿Trabajan ustedes diez horas?
16 ¿Tienen mucho dinero?

Now think up your own answers. Yours may be different from mine but quite correct.

17 ¿A qué hora va usted a Barcelona?
18 ¿Qué tal las tostadas?
19 ¿Dónde está 'Casa Margarita'?
20 ¿Hay servicios aquí? ¿Y dónde están?

Answers

1 ¿Tiene (usted) una habitación?
2 Es un poco grande.
3 ¿A qué hora es el desayuno?
4 Los ordenadores son caros.
5 Quisiéramos comer algo.
6 ¿Cuánto cuesta el té?
7 ¿Dónde está la cafetería? ¿A la derecha?
8 Vamos a Málaga a las dos.
9 Perdone, la cuenta, por favor.
10 ¿Hay un banco aquí cerca?
11 Sí, tengo una tarjeta Visa.
12 Sí, hay un bar aquí.
13 Sí, es una cuenta muy grande.
14 No, no estamos de vacaciones.
15 No, no trabajamos diez horas.
16 No, no tenemos mucho dinero.
17 Voy a Barcelona a las tres y media.
18 Las tostadas están buenas, pero frías.
19 'Casa Margarita' está en Sierra Nevada.
20 Sí, hay servicios aquí. Están todo recto.

If you managed to get more than half right the first time, give yourself a pat on the back.

Let's speak more Spanish

🔊 CD1, tr 15

Here are the two optional exercises. Remember, they may stretch the 35 minutes a day by an extra 15 minutes. But the extra practice will be worth it.

In your own words

This exercise will teach you to express yourself freely. Use only the words you have learned so far.

Ask me in your own words…

1 if an en suite double room is available
2 what the price of the room is for one night
3 where you can have a coffee
4 if the café is straight ahead and on the left or on the right

Tell me…

5 you would like breakfast at 7.30
6 you are thinking of driving to Barcelona the next day
7 you want coffee and toast
8 what you don't like about the café
9 what Kate likes about the café (**dice** (*she says*):…)
10 that the bill is €9.10

Answers

1 ¿Tiene usted una habitación doble con baño o con ducha?
2 ¿Cuánto cuesta la habitación para una noche?
3 ¿Dónde hay una cafetería aquí cerca?
4 La cafetería ¿está todo recto y a la izquierda o a la derecha?
5 Quisiera el desayuno a las siete y media.
6 Quisiera ir a Barcelona mañana.
7 Quisiera café y tostadas.
8 La mesa no está limpia y la tostada está mala.
9 Kate dice: 'Los servicios son estupendos; el camarero es muy guapo.'
10 La cuenta es nueve euros y diez céntimos.

Let's speak Spanish – fast and fluently

🔊 CD1, tr 16

No more stuttering and stumbling! Get out the stopwatch and time yourself with this fluency practice. Translate each section and check if it is correct, then cover up the answers and say the three or four sentences fast!

Good evening, do you have a room with bath?
*80 (**ochenta**) euros is a little expensive.*
I would like a room with shower.
How much is (costs) the breakfast?

Buenas noches. ¿Tiene usted una habitación con baño?
Ochenta euros es un poco caro.
Quisiera una habitación con ducha.
¿Cuánto cuesta el desayuno?

My company is here very near, straight ahead, on the left.
But I am going tomorrow to Valencia.
I would like to go at 9.30.

Mi empresa está aquí muy cerca, todo recto, a la izquierda.
Pero voy mañana a Valencia.
Quisiera ir a las nueve y media.

The café here is very small and expensive.
The toilets are not clean.
The coffee is cold and there is no tea.
The bill? Two tapas – eight euros.

La cafetería aquí es muy pequeña y cara.
Los servicios no están limpios.
El café está frío y no hay té.
¿La cuenta? Dos tapas – ocho euros.

Now say all the sentences in Spanish without stopping and starting.

Test your progress

Translate these sentences into Spanish and write them down.

See what you can remember without looking at the previous pages.

1 Where is there a telephone? On the right?
2 Can we eat some toast here? Are there seats for four?
3 Do you have a table? At half past eight? We are six.
4 Let's go to the cafeteria, all right?
5 Can you repair the Seat? It has broken down.
6 We are in the room. Where are you?
7 The tapas are excellent. I can eat lots.
8 Can I ask you? You have a small company. Is it in Texas?
9 We cannot go on holiday in July. We do not have money.
10 Where is the waiter? Does he have my bill?
11 Where are the toilets? On the left?
12 Maria and I would like to go to Granada – without husbands.
13 Excuse me, I have only €35 and a credit card.
14 €3.10 for a cold tortilla? It is very expensive.
15 I have been in Seville for one night. It costs less in November.
16 Mrs López is very good-looking. Where does she work? Very near?
17 Agreed! We take the Seat for April.
18 London is not pretty in November.
19 I have worked a little with computers. It is not easy.
20 At what time are we going to be here? At one.

Check your answers and remember the scoring instructions.
Then enter your result on the **Progress chart**.

Week 3
Day-by-day guide

Study for 35 minutes a day – but there are no penalties for doing more!

Day one
- Read **Let's go shopping**.
- Listen to/Read **Vamos de compras**.
- Read the **New words**, then learn some of them.

Day two
- Repeat **Vamos de compras** and the **New words**.
- Learn all the **New words**. Use the **Flash cards**!

Day three
- Test yourself on all the **New words** – boring, boring, but you are over half way already
- Listen to/Read **Spot the keys**.
- Learn the **Good news grammar**.

Day four
- Go over the **Good news grammar**.
- Cut out and learn the ten **Flash sentences**.

Day five
- Listen to/Read **Let's speak Spanish**.
- Listen to/Read **Learn by heart**.

Day six
- Go over **Learn by heart**.
- Have a quick look at the **New words** Weeks 1–3. You know 226 words by now! Well, more or less.
- Listen to/Read **Let's speak more Spanish** (optional).
- Listen to/Read **Let's speak Spanish – fast and fluently** (optional).
- Translate **Test your progress**.

Day seven – Enjoy your day off.

Let's go shopping

Next stop Marbella and a week in a holiday apartment. Kate plans to do some shopping but Tom is less keen.

Kate   Well, today we must go shopping. Are we going to the (town) centre?

Tom   But it makes bad weather. It makes cold and there is football and tennis in the television… and golf at twelve and half…

Kate   I am sorry but first we must go to a cash dispenser and to a tobacconist or to the post office to buy stamps…and then to the chemist's and the dry cleaner's.

Tom   And so not there is golf... perhaps football at three o'clock... Is that all?

Kate   No, we must go to El Corte Inglés to buy a suitcase new and I have to go to a supermarket and to the hairdresser. And then I would like to buy some shoes.

Tom   Good grief! Until what hour are open the shops?

Kate   I believe (that) until 8 o'clock.

Tom   And so there is not football… perhaps tennis at eight and quarter.

(Later)

Kate   I believe that I have bought too much; a quarter of a kilo of ham, half kilo of cheese, 200 grams of pâté, eggs, bread, butter, sugar, six beers and a bottle of wine red.

Tom   It doesn't matter. There is enough for two days. Not we have eaten anything since yesterday. And what is there in the bag big? Something for me?

Kate   Well, I have gone to the hairdresser of El Corte Inglés and afterwards I have seen some shoes in blue. They are great, aren't they? The sales assistant was very nice and handsome like Tom Cruise.

Tom   Who is Tom Cruise? And how much cost the shoes?

Kate   They were a little expensive…€100… It is the same price in England!

Tom   What? My wife is mad!

Kate   But this T-shirt of golf size 50, was very cheap, only €10, and here I have a newspaper English and is there not now tennis in the television?

Vamos de compras

🔊 CD1, tr 17

Next stop Marbella and a week in a holiday apartment. Kate plans to do some shopping but Tom is less keen.

Kate   Pues… hoy tenemos que ir de compras. ¿Vamos al centro?

Tom   Pero hace mal tiempo. Hace frío, y hay fútbol y tenis en la tele… y golf a las doce y media…

Kate   Lo siento, pero primero tenemos que ir a un cajero, y a un estanco o a correos para comprar sellos… y después a la farmacia y a la tintorería.

Tom   Entonces, no hay golf… quizás fútbol a las tres…¿Es eso todo?

Kate   No, tenemos que ir al Corte Inglés a comprar una maleta nueva, y yo tengo que ir a un supermercado y a la peluquería. Y luego quisiera comprar unos zapatos.

Tom   ¡Madre mía! ¿Hasta qué hora están abiertas las tiendas?

Kate   Creo que hasta las ocho.

Tom   Entonces, no hay fútbol… quizás tenis a las ocho y cuarto…

(Más tarde)

Kate   Creo que he comprado demasiado: un cuarto de kilo de jamón, medio kilo de queso, 200 gramos de paté, huevos, pan, mantequilla, azúcar, seis cervezas y una botella de vino tinto.

Tom   No importa. Hay bastante para dos días. No hemos comido nada desde ayer. Y ¿qué hay en la bolsa grande? ¿Algo para mí?

Kate   Pues, he ido a la peluquería del El Corte Inglés y después he visto unos zapatos en azul. Son estupendos ¿verdad? El dependiente era muy amable y guapo, como Tom Cruise.

Tom   ¿Quién es Tom Cruise? Y ¿cuánto cuestan los zapatos?

Kate   Eran un poco caros… cien euros…¡Es el mismo precio que en Inglaterra!

Tom   ¿Qué? ¡Mi mujer está loca!

Kate   Pero esta camiseta de golf talla 50, era muy barata, sólo diez euros, y aquí tengo un periódico inglés y ¿no hay ahora tenis en la tele?

New words

🔊 CD1, tr 18

Learn the new words in half the time by using the **Flash cards**. There are 22 to start you off.

hoy today
tenemos que we have to, we must
ir de compras go shopping
al centro to the centre
hace mal tiempo it is bad weather (lit. it makes…)
hace frío it is cold (lit. it makes cold)
el fútbol the football
la tele, la televisión the TV
lo siento I'm sorry
primero first
un cajero (automático) a cashpoint machine
el estanco the tobacconist
correos the post office
comprar (to) buy
los sellos the stamps
después afterwards, then
la farmacia the chemist's
la tintorería the dry cleaner's
entonces and so
quizás perhaps
ese, esa/eso (by itself) that
todo all
El Corte Inglés (a Spanish chain of department stores)
una maleta suitcase
nuevo/a new

tengo que I have to, must
un supermercado a supermarket
la peluquería the hairdresser's
los zapatos the shoes
¡Madre mía! good grief! (lit. my mother!)
hasta until
abierto open
la tienda the shop
creo I believe
que that, as
más more
más tarde later
he comprado I have bought, I bought
demasiado too, too much
el jamón the ham
el queso the cheese
un gramo a gram
los huevos the eggs
el pan the bread
la mantequilla the butter
el azúcar the sugar
la cerveza the beer
una botella a bottle
el vino tinto the red wine
no importa it doesn't matter, no problem
bastante enough, rather
hemos comido we have eaten

nada nothing
desde since
ayer yesterday
la bolsa/el bolso the bag/the handbag
para mí for me
he ido I have gone
he visto I have seen
azul blue
¿verdad? isn't it, aren't they, don't you, etc.
el dependiente the sales assistant
era he/she/it was, I was
amable kind, charming

como like, as
¿quién? who?
eran they were
el mismo the same
el precio the price
cien a hundred
Inglaterra England
loco/a crazy
este, esta/esto (by itself) this
la camiseta the T-shirt
la talla the size
barato/a cheap
un periódico a newspaper
ingles English

> TOTAL NEW WORDS: 78
> … only 167 words to go!

Some easy extras

Los colores *(The colours)*

blanco/a white
negro/a black
rojo/a red
azul blue
verde green

amarillo/a yellow
marrón brown
gris grey
naranja orange
rosa pink

Spot the keys

◀) CD1, tr 19

By now you can say many things in Spanish. But what happens if you ask a question and do not understand the answer? Don't panic; just listen for the words you know. Any familiar words which you pick up will provide you with key words – clues to what the other person is saying. If you have the recording, close the book now, listen to the dialogue and write down all the key words you have recognized.

Here's an example:

You   Perdone, quisiera ir a correos. ¿Dónde está?

Answer   *Pues, esmuysencillo: siga* **todo recto hasta** *el siguiente cruceconsemáforos. Hay algunosedificios, entreellos* **una casa roja a la izquierda**. *Después hay una residenciadeancianos y* **unas tiendas. A la derecha** *hay una* **tintorería.** *Atraviese* **el parking** *y verálaoficina* **de correos.**

Despite a lot of words running into each other, hopefully you managed to pick out: **todo recto – hasta – una casa roja – a la izquierda – unas tiendas – a la derecha – tintorería – el parking – de correos.**

Good news grammar

🔊 CD1, tr 20

1 The past

Imagine you were getting married today. You would say *I do*.
If it happened yesterday you would say *I did* or *I have done it*. When
you want to talk about the past in Spanish the easiest way is to use
haber, another kind of *have* (never **tener**) plus a changed main verb.
For example, **trabajar** becomes **trabajado** and **comprar** becomes
comprado. Let's put it together.

I bought or *I have bought*	**he comprado**
you (sing.) *bought* or *you have bought*	**ha comprado**
he/she/it bought or *has bought*	**ha comprado**
we bought or *we have bought*	**hemos comprado**
they bought or *they have bought*	**han comprado**
you (plural) *bought* or *have bought*	**han comprado**

Not all verbs are so well behaved and just change to **-ado**. Here are
three odd ones which you'll use all the time.

ir	*(to go)*	but:	**he ido**	*I went, I have gone*
ver	*(to see)*	but:	**he visto**	*I saw, I have seen*
tener	*(to have)*	but:	**he tenido**	*I had, I have had*

If you get confused have a sneak preview of Week 6. There's a
complete list of all the verbs in this book. You'll find that you
know lots already.

2 A + el = al; de + el = del

a and **de** plus **el** are always contracted to **al** and **del**.

Vamos *al* centro. *We go **to the** centre.*
cinco minutos *del* bar *five minutes **from the** bar*

3 *Tener que:* must, have to

How often do you say *I have to* or *I must?*

Tengo que trabajar. *I must work. I have to work.*

Tenemos que comprar. *We have to buy. We must buy.*

¿Tiene usted que ir? *Do you have to go? Must you go?*

Don't forget the **que!**

4 *Ir* (go) and *poder* (can)

You know the routine. Practise saying the verbs until you can say them with your eyes closed.

	I	*you/he/she/it*	we	*they/you*
ir	**voy**	**va**	**vamos**	**van**
poder	**puedo**	**puede**	**podemos**	**pueden**

Let's speak Spanish

🔊 CD2, tr 1

If you have the recording, listen to check your answers. Say each sentence one at a time – out loud.

1 I am sorry, I have to go.
2 We would like to go shopping.
3 Where are there shops?
4 At what time are they open?
5 I would like to buy bread.
6 Today it is very cold.
7 Good grief! Did you see it?
8 We have to buy beer.
9 We have eaten at (in) El Corte Inglés.
10 You don't have (a) TV? It doesn't matter.

Answer these questions using the *I* form and the words in brackets.

11 ¿Qué ha comprado? (un periódico inglés)
12 ¿Dónde ha comprado esto? (en el supermercado)
13 ¿Qué ha visto? (muchas tiendas)
14 ¿Qué ha comido? (una paella)
15 ¿Cuántas horas ha trabajado? (ocho horas)

Now answer these questions with **No** and the *we* form of the verb.

16 ¿Han ido al fútbol?
17 ¿Han comprado la tele?
18 ¿Tienen que ir a correos?
19 ¿Van al centro?
20 Finally, make up a giant sentence without drawing breath using

ahora – centro – Seat – mi amiga – tienda – comprar – zapatos – mi marido. Start with: **Ahora…**

Answers

1 Lo siento, tengo que ir.
2 Quisiéramos ir de compras.
3 ¿Dónde hay tiendas?
4 ¿A qué hora están abiertas?
5 Quisiera comprar pan.
6 Hoy hace mucho frío.
7 ¡Madre mía! ¿Lo ha visto?
8 Tenemos que comprar cerveza.
9 Hemos comido en El Corte Inglés.
10 ¿No tiene tele? No importa.
11 He comprado un periódico inglés.
12 He comprado esto en el supermercado. *or* Lo he comprado…
13 He visto muchas tiendas.
14 He comido una paella.
15 He trabajado ocho horas.
16 No, no hemos ido al fútbol.
17 No, no hemos comprado la tele.
18 No, no tenemos que ir a correos.
19 No, no vamos al centro.
20 Ahora voy al centro en el Seat con mi amiga a la tienda a comprar zapatos para mi marido.

Let's speak more Spanish

🔊 CD2, tr 2

For these optional exercises add an extra 15 minutes to your daily schedule. And remember, don't worry about getting the article or endings wrong. Near enough is good enough!

In your own words

This exercise will teach you to express yourself freely. Use only the words you have learned so far.

Tell me in your own words that...

1 you would like to do the shopping today
2 you are aiming for the middle of the town
3 you are out of cash
4 you have to go first to a cashpoint machine.
5 then you have to go to the pharmacy
6 you have seen a shoe shop
7 you have to buy new shoes
8 you bought shoes, and they weren't cheap
9 you did not get much in the supermarket
10 you bought bread and butter, and a little white wine – ten bottles.

Answers

1 **Quisiera ir de compras hoy.**
2 **Voy al centro.**
3 **No tengo dinero.**
4 **Primero tengo que ir a un cajero...**
5 **Después tengo que ir a la farmacia.**
6 **He visto una tienda de zapatos.**
7 **Tengo que comprar zapatos nuevos.**
8 **He comprado zapatos, y no eran baratos.**
9 **No he comprado mucho en el supermercado.**
10 **He comprado pan y mantequilla y un poco de vino blanco – diez botellas.**

Let's speak Spanish – fast and fluently

◀)) CD2, tr 3

Translate each section and check if it is correct, then cover up the answers and say the three or four sentences fast!

Excuse me, are you buying a television?
Is it expensive, the blue television?
No, not too much, in England it is the same price.

¿Perdone, compra usted una tele?
¿Es cara la tele azul?
No, no demasiado, en Inglaterra es el mismo precio.

I would like to buy a suitcase, but not too expensive.
We have a suitcase, but it is too small.
I have seen a suitcase, and it is rather big.

Quisiera comprar una maleta, pero no demasiado cara.
Tenemos una maleta, pero es demasiado pequeña.
He visto una maleta, y es bastante grande.

The weather is very bad in April.
We went to Madrid. We have eaten at (en) El Corte Inglés.
Ham, cheese and bread – the bill was 10 euros.
The waiter wasn't handsome but he was very nice.

Hace mal tiempo en abril.
Hemos ido a Madrid. Hemos comido en El Corte Inglés.
Jamón, queso y pan – la cuenta era diez euros.
El camarero no era guapo pero era muy amable.

Now say all the sentences in Spanish without stopping and starting. Try to do it in under one minute.

If you are not happy with your result – just try once more.

Learn by heart

🔊 CD2, tr 4

Try to say this dialogue in under one minute! The more expression you use when saying it, the easier it will be to remember it.

Vamos de compras

A Hoy tenemos que ir de compras – vamos al centro.

B Pero hace frío…

A ¡No importa!

B ¡Madre mía! ¡No tengo dinero! ¿Dónde hay un cajero?

A Creo que he comprado demasiado: pan, mantequilla, jamón y queso… y seis botellas de vino blanco.

B ¿Y las cervezas?

A Ah…¡lo siento!

Test your progress

Translate the following sentences in writing. Then check the answers and be amazed by your progress.

1 We can buy stamps at (in) the tobacconist's, can't we?
2 Did you see the tennis on the TV? Yes, I have seen everything.
3 She was very kind, as always.
4 Good grief! The eggs are broken! It doesn't matter.
5 Yesterday was a rather good day.
6 The English newspaper was not cheap.
7 I believe that I have seen a dry cleaner in El Corte Inglés.
8 Until what time do you have to work? Until eight?
9 At what time do we have to go? I cannot go until later.
10 In November it is always bad weather in Manchester.
11 What did you buy? Six bottles of red wine? Great!
12 Size 44: what is that in English? Perhaps 14.
13 It is very cold in this house. I must buy something.
14 First I went shopping and then we ate with friends.
15 We have had the new TV since yesterday. And today it is broken.
16 You have bought a black case, not red, haven't you?
17 Everything was very expensive. So then we did not buy anything.
18 Who is the sales assistant? Where is the milk?
19 We do not have the T-shirt in green and at the same price.
20 I would like to buy something for me. But not too expensive.

Remember to fill in the **Progress chart.** You are now halfway there.

Week 4

Day-by-day guide

Study 35 minutes a day but if you are keen try 40 or even 45.

Day one
- Read **We're going to eat out**.
- Listen to/Read **Vamos a comer**.
- Read the **New words**. Learn the easy ones.

Day two
- Repeat the dialogue. Learn the harder **New words**.
- Cut out the **Flash words** to help you.

Day three
- Learn all the **New words** until you know them well.
- Read and learn the **Good news grammar**.

Day four
- Cut out and learn the **Flash sentences**.
- Listen to/Read **Learn by heart**.

Day five
- Read **Say it simply**.
- Listen to/Read **Let's speak Spanish**.

Day six
- Listen to/Read **Spot the keys**.
- Listen to/Read **Let's speak more Spanish** (optional).
- Listen to/Read **Let's speak Spanish – fast and fluently** (optional).
- Translate **Test your progress**.

Day seven – Are you keeping your scores above 60%? If so, have a well-earned day off.

We're going to eat out

Tom and Kate are off to dinner with an important client. Will Kate be able to handle the infamous Edith?

No more 'Spanglish!' As you'll have realized by now not everything can be translated word for word from one language to the other. If you simply exchange the words people may understand you and might even be amused, but saying things the Spanish way will sound much better and will impress the locals.

Kate   Tom, somebody from Madrid has telephoned. He didn't say why (for what). I don't have the number, (it is that) at that moment I didn't have paper. A name like Gámez or Gálvez.

Tom   Ah yes, Juan Gálvez, a good client of the company. I know him well. He is very nice. I have an appointment with him on Tuesday. This is for an important matter.

Tom   *(On the phone)* Hello, good morning Mr Gálvez. This is Tom Walker… Yes, thank you… yes, sure, that is possible… on Tuesday, next week… correct… that's all right… yes, very interesting… no, we have time… great… no, only some days… oh yes… when?… at nine… upstairs, at the exit… in front of the door. And so, until tonight, thank you very much, until later.

Kate   What are we doing this evening?

Tom   We are going to eat with Mr Gálvez, in the centre, behind the church. He says that the restaurant is new and very good. He is in Marbella for two days with Edith and Peter Palmer from our company.

Kate   I know Edith Palmer. I do not like her. She is boring and very snobbish. She has a terrible dog. I believe that I am going to be ill tonight. A cold with aches. The doctor must come.

Tom   No, please! Mr Gálvez is an important client. One cannot do that.

(In the restaurant: Luis explains the menu.)

Luis   The fish is not on the menu, and the dessert today is ice cream of the house.

Juan   Mrs Walker, what do you like? Perhaps a soup… and afterwards?

Vamos a comer

🔊 CD2, tr 5

Tom and Kate are off to dinner with an important client. Will Kate be able to handle the infamous Edith?

Kate   Tom, alguien de Madrid ha llamado. No ha dicho para qué. No tengo el número, es que en ese momento no he tenido papel. Un nombre como Gámez o Gálvez.

Tom   Ah, sí, Juan Gálvez, un buen cliente de la empresa. Lo conozco bien. Es muy amable. Tengo una cita con él, el martes. Esto es para una cosa importante.

Tom   *(Al teléfono)* Hola, buenos días Señor Gálvez. Soy Tom Walker… Sí, gracias… sí, seguro, eso es posible… el martes, la semana que viene,… correcto… está bien… sí, muy interesante… no, tenemos tiempo… estupendo… no, sólo unos días… ah sí…¿cuándo?… a las nueve… arriba, a la salida… delante de la puerta… Entonces, hasta esta noche, muchas gracias, hasta luego.

Kate   ¿Qué hacemos esta noche?

Tom   Vamos a comer con el Señor Gálvez, en el centro, detrás de la iglesia. Dice que el restaurante es nuevo y muy bueno. Está en Marbella durante dos días, con Edith y Peter Palmer de nuestra empresa.

Kate   Conozco a Edith Palmer. Ella no me gusta. Es aburrida y muy esnob. Tiene un perro terrible. Creo que esta noche voy a estar enferma. Un resfriado y dolores. El doctor tiene que venir.

Tom   ¡No, por favor! El Señor Gálvez es un cliente importante. Eso no se puede hacer.

(En el restaurante: Luis explica el menú.)

Luis   El pescado no está en el menú, y el postre hoy es helado de la casa.

Juan   Señora Walker, ¿qué le gusta? Quizá una sopa…¿y después?

Kate	Well… a steak with salad, please.
Edith	Too much red meat is not good for you.
Juan	Mr Walker? Do you like (the) lamb? And what would you like to drink?
Tom	Right… lamb chops for me with chips and vegetables – but all without garlic – and a beer, please.
Edith	Tom, garlic is very good for you. And I like it very much.
Juan	And you, Mrs Palmer?
Edith	A little roast chicken, a glass of still water, please.
(Later)	
Juan	Have we finished? Does anyone want dessert… fruit… a coffee? Nobody? Well then, the bill, please.
Edith	Ah, Señor Gálvez, could you help me, please? How do you say 'doggy bag' in Spanish? I would like a bag for my dog.
Kate	But Edith, the dog is in England!

Kate   Pues… un filete con ensalada, por favor.

Edith   Demasiada carne roja no es bueno para usted.

Juan   Señor Walker, ¿le gusta el cordero? ¿Y qué quiere usted para beber?

Tom   Bueno, para mí chuletas de cordero con patatas fritas y verdura – pero todo sin ajo – y una cerveza, por favor.

Edith   Tom, el ajo es muy bueno para usted. Y a mí me gusta mucho.

Juan   ¿Y usted, Señora Palmer?

Edith   Un poco de pollo asado, un vaso de agua sin gas, por favor.

(Más tarde)

Juan   ¿Hemos terminado? ¿Alguien quiere un postre… fruta… un café? ¿Nadie? Bueno, la cuenta, por favor.

Edith   Ah, Señor Gálvez, ¿podría ayudarme, por favor? ¿Cómo se dice 'doggy bag' en español? Quisiera una bolsa para mi perro.

Kate   Pero Edith, ¡el perro está en Inglaterra!

New words

◀ CD2, tr 6

alguien someone
ha llamado has called
ha dicho has said
es que... it is that, that's because...
el papel the paper
el nombre the name
el cliente the client
conozco (a) I know (usually somebody or a place)
bien well, all right
una cita an appointment
él he, him
martes Tuesday
una cosa a thing, a matter
importante important
gracias, muchas gracias thank you, thank you very much
seguro (de) sure (about)
posible possible
la semana que viene next week (the week that comes)
correcto correct
interesante interesting
tiempo time, also: weather
arriba above, upstairs
la salida the exit
delante (de) in front of
la puerta the door
hacemos we do
detrás (de) behind
la iglesia the church
dice he/she/it says, you say
el restaurante the restaurant
durante during, for

nuestro/a our
me gusta/no me gusta I like (it)/I do not like (it)
esnob snobbish
un perro a dog
terrible terrible
enfermo sick, ill
un resfriado a cold
el dolor the pain, ache
el doctor the doctor
venir (to) come
puedo, puede I can, he/she/it/you can
no se puede hacer one cannot do that
el pescado the fish
el menu the menu
el postre the dessert
helado ice cream
le gusta you like, do you like?
una sopa a soup
un filete a fillet steak
una ensalada a salad
la carne the meat
el cordero the lamb
¿qué quiere? what do you want?
beber (to) drink
las chuletas the chops
las patatas fritas the chips
la verdura the vegetables
el ajo the garlic
el pollo asado the roast chicken
la fruta the fruit
un vaso a glass

el agua (f.) the water
con/sin gas carbonated/
  non-carbonated
terminado finished
nadie nobody

¿podría ayudarme? could you
  help me?
¿cómo…? how…?
¿cómo se dice en español…? how
  does one say in Spanish…?

TOTAL NEW WORDS: 69
… only 98 words to go!

Some more easy extras
Los días de la semana *(days of the week)*
lunes *Monday*
martes *Tuesday*
miércoles *Wednesday*
jueves *Thursday*
viernes *Friday*
sábado *Saturday*
domingo *Sunday*

Good news grammar

🔊 CD2, tr 7

1 The future

There is an easy way to say something that is going to happen in the future. You don't use *shall* or *will* but simply *going to*.

Vamos a comprar pan. *We are going to buy bread.*

2 Me gusta – no me gusta

I like – I don't like – do you like…? You'll use this a lot! In Spanish **gusta** is a bit of a strange construction. Think of it as saying that something pleases you.

***me gusta* el vino**	*I like the wine*
***le gusta* el Seat**	*you like the Seat*
***le gusta* el pan**	*he/she likes the bread*
***nos gusta* la casa**	*we like the house*
***les gusta* la fruta**	*they like the fruit*

If you do not like something simply add **no**:

No me gusta el vino/El vino no me gusta. *I do not like the wine.*

When you like or do not like more than one thing use **gustan**:

Las patatas fritas me gustan mucho. *I like the chips.*

No me gustan las vacaciones. *I don't like the holidays.*

3 *Conozco a Edith* I know Edith

When a verb is followed by a direct object which is a person you have to slip in an **a**.

He visto a Pepe. *I have seen Pepe.*

4 *Comer* and *querer*

Spend five minutes on each verb so that you can use it without having to look them up.

Comer is a team player. Many verbs ending in **-er** have endings like him. **Querer** is a rebel. But you'll need **quisiera**… every day.

comer *(to eat)*		querer *(to) wish, want*	
como	*I eat*	**quisiera**	*I would like*
come	*you eat*	**quisiera**	*you would like*
come	*he, she, it eats*	**quisiera**	*he/she/it would like*
comemos	*we eat*	**quisiéramos**	*we would like*
comen	*they, you eat*	**quisieran**	*they/you would like*

5 Last easy extras: more numbers and time
los números

11 **once**	*19* **diecinueve**	*50* **cincuenta**
12 **doce**	*20* **veinte**	*60* **sesenta**
13 **trece**	*21* **veintiuno/a**	*70* **setenta**
14 **catorce**	*22* **veintidós**	*80* **ochenta**
15 **quince**	*23* **veintitrés**	*90* **noventa**
16 **dieciséis**	*30* **treinta**	*100* **cien**
17 **diecisiete**	*31* **treinta y uno/a** (etc.)	*200* **doscientos/as**
18 **dieciocho**	*40* **cuarenta**	*500* **quinientos**
		1,000 **mil**

¿Qué hora es? *(What's the time?)*

¿a qué hora?	*at what time?*	**a las cinco**	*at five o'clock*
es la una	*it is one o'clock*	**son las dos**	*it is two o'clock*
un minuto	*a minute*	**una hora**	*an hour*
un día	*a day*	**una semana**	*a week*
un mes	*a month*	**un año**	*a year*

Learn by heart

◀) CD2, tr 8

Here is someone who is rather fed up. Act it out in 45 seconds!

> **No me gusta…**
>
> **A** ¿Conoce* al Señor Gómez? Es un buen cliente de la empresa. Tengo que ir a comer con él.
>
> **B** ¿Ah sí?
>
> **A** No me gusta. No es amable. Come mucho y bebe más.
>
> **B** ¿Y cuándo?
>
> **A** ¡Esta noche! Hay fútbol en la tele. Quisiera tener un resfriado pero eso no se puede hacer…¡Siempre la empresa!
>
> **B** ¡Lo siento!
>
> *¿**Conoce…?** *Do you know…?*

Say it simply

When people want to speak Spanish but don't dare, it's usually because they are trying to translate what they want to say from English into Spanish. And when they don't know some of the words, they give up.

With **Fast Spanish with Elisabeth Smith** you work around the words you don't know with the words you do know! Believe me, with 393 words you can say anything! It may not always be very elegant, but you are communicating.

Here are two examples showing you how to say things in a simple way. Words that are not part of the vocabulary have been highlighted.

1 You need to **change** your **flight** from Tuesday to Friday.

Saying it simply:

> **No podemos ir el martes, quisieramos ir el viernes.**
> *We cannot go on Tuesday, we would like to go on Friday.*

or: **No es posible ir el martes, tenemos que ir el viernes.**
It is not possible to go on Tuesday, we have to go on Friday.

2 You want to get your purse from the coach which the driver has locked.

Saying it simply:

> **Lo siento, tengo que ir en el bus. Mi dinero está en el bus.**
> *I am sorry, I have to go in(to) the bus. My money is in the bus.*

or: **Tengo que tener mi dinero. Desgraciadamente todo está en el bus.**
I have to have my money. Unfortunately everything is in the bus.

Say it simply – in the past

Here are eight essential verbs for when you want to talk about the past – simply.

estar	*to be*	**he estado**	*I was, I have been*
comer	*to eat*	**he comido**	*I ate, I have eaten*
venir	*to come*	**he venido**	*I came, I have come*
hacer	*to do*	**he hecho**	*I did, I have done*
decir	*to say*	**he dicho**	*I said, I have said*
dar	*to give*	**he dado**	*I gave, I have given*
saber	*to know (a fact)*	**he sabido**	*I knew, I have known*
escribir	*to write*	**he escrito**	*I wrote, I have written*

Let's speak Spanish

🔊 CD2, tr 9

Here are ten sentences as a warm-up! Listen to the recording
if you have it.

1 I do not like the client.
2 Do we go with him?
3 What do you want, the meat or the fish?
4 Yes, sure, I would like to go home.
5 Do you have an appointment for me?
6 I like going to Mallorca.
7 Who has said that?
8 Has someone called?
9 I know a cheap restaurant.
10 Can you help me, please?

Now pretend you are in Spain with friends who do not speak Spanish.
They want you to ask someone things and will want you to do it for
them in Spanish. They will say: *Please ask him…*

11 if he knows Edith Palmer.
12 if he likes lamb.
13 what he wants to drink.
14 if he has time next week.
15 if he has dogs.

On another occasion your friends ask you to tell someone things.
They say: *Please tell her…* If you don't know the odd word work
round it by using the ones you do.

16 the soup is stone cold.
17 that he/she is a vegetarian.
18 that we are in a rush now.
19 that nobody has seen him.
20 that he/she cannot go tomorrow.

Answers

1 No me gusta el cliente.
2 ¿Vamos con él?
3 ¿Qué quiere, la carne o el pescado?
4 Sí, seguro, quisiera ir a casa.
5 ¿Tiene una cita para mí?
6 Me gusta ir a Mallorca.
7 ¿Quién ha dicho eso?
8 ¿Ha llamado alguien?
9 Conozco un restaurante barato.
10 ¿Puede ayudarme, por favor?
11 ¿Conoce a Edith Palmer?
12 ¿Le gusta el cordero?
13 ¿Qué quiere beber?
14 ¿Tiene tiempo la semana que viene?
15 ¿Tiene perros?
16 Lo siento, pero la sopa está muy fría.
17 Él/Ella no come carne.
18 Lo siento, pero no tenemos tiempo ahora.
19 Nadie lo ha visto.
20 Él/Ella no puede ir mañana.

Let's speak more Spanish

🔊 CD2, tr 10

In your own words

This exercise will teach you to express yourself freely. Use only the words you have learned so far.

Tell me in your own words that…

1 somebody has the number of Carlos López
2 you spoke with him on the phone
3 he says he goes to Madrid on Friday
4 he is a very important and good client
5 you believe that you have an appointment with him next week
6 you are going out to eat with Carlos on Saturday
7 Edith Palmer cannot make it – she has a cold
8 you are very fond of tortilla and paella
9 nobody is eating fruit or cheese
10 you went to the restaurant at half past eleven

Answers

1 **Alguien tiene el número de Carlos López.**
2 **He hablado con él por teléfono.**
3 **Dice que va a Madrid el viernes.**
4 **Es un cliente muy importante y bueno.**
5 **Creo que tengo una cita con él la semana que viene.**
6 **Voy a comer con Carlos el sábado.**
7 **Edith Palmer no puede ir – tiene un resfriado.**
8 **Me gustan mucho la tortilla y la paella.**
9 **Nadie come fruta o queso.**
10 **He ido al restaurante a las once y media.**

Let's speak Spanish – fast and fluently

🔊 CD2, tr 11

Translate each section into Spanish and check if it is correct, then cover up the answers and say the three or four sentences as quickly and correctly as possible.

If you manage to say each section in less than 20 seconds give yourself a pat on the back.

Some of the English is in 'Spanish-speak' to help you.

Do you know Carlos López? He phoned today.
Why? He said it was important.
It was for an appointment on Wednesday.

¿Conoce a Carlos López? Ha llamado hoy.
¿Por qué? Ha dicho que era importante.
Era para una cita el miércoles.

Carlos is only until (the) Friday in Bilbao.
There is a restaurant. It is new, behind the bank.
But I would like to eat with him at my house tonight.

Carlos está en Bilbao sólo hasta el viernes.
Hay un restaurante. Es nuevo, detrás del banco.
Pero quisiera comer con él en mi casa esta noche.

Unfortunately, I cannot go.
My dog is ill. He has pains. He has eaten too much meat.
Oh, I am sorry. How do you say in Spanish: 'Poor little thing?'

Desgraciadamente no puedo ir.
Mi perro está enfermo. Tiene dolores. Ha comido demasiada carne.
Oh, lo siento. ¿Cómo se dice en español: 'Poor little thing'?
('Pobrecito'.)

Now say all the sentences in Spanish without stopping and starting.

Spot the keys

🔊 CD2, tr 12

You practised listening for key words when you asked the way to the post office in Week 3. Now you are in a department store and you ask the sales assistant if the black shoes you liked are also available in size 39:

Perdone, ¿tiene estos zapatos también en número treinta y nueve?

She said **no** then **un momento, por favor** and disappeared. When she came back this is what she said:

Acabo de mirar en el almacén y he llamado a otra sucursal, pero tienen los **zapatos sólo en marrón**. *Pero sé por experiencia que esta marca* **siempre viene en tallas muy grandes** *y en mi opinión el* **número treinta y ocho** *sería* **bastante grande**.

Size 39 was only available in brown but size 38 might be big enough.

Test your progress

1 What did he say? He said: For whom are the chips?
2 Can you come to our house? Next week?
3 She says that the exit of the shop is upstairs behind the bar.
4 Did you say that he has gone to England?
5 What do you want? It is that… I am sick and I cannot work.
6 Could you help me, please? Is there a doctor here?
7 Is he going to the appointment without shoes? One cannot do that.
8 I know Isabel Romero. She is a very interesting woman.
9 Nobody can drink 15 beers in one night. It is not possible.
10 I like (the) dessert very much. I would like the ice cream.
11 He says that it is an important matter, but he has no time.
12 We have finished and now we must go to Valencia.
13 I eat a lot of salads. What do you eat?
14 How do you like the fish? Without garlic?
15 The name of this vegetable: how does one say in Spanish…?
16 There are no shops in front of the church or behind. What do we do?
17 The company called. A Mr López said that it is an important matter.
18 I am sure they have carbonated water. They always have it.
19 He says that he has pains since yesterday. Do you believe it?
20 I have a cold. I cannot go to England today.

If you are happy with your result take it straight to the
Progress chart.

Week 5

Day-by-day guide

How about 15 minutes on the train, tube or bus, ten minutes on the way home and 20 minutes before switching on the television…?

Day one
- Read **On the move**.
- Listen to/Read **De acá para allá**.
- Read the **New words**. Learn 15 or more.

Day two
- Repeat **De acá para allá** and the **New words**.
- Cut out the **Flash words** and get stuck in.

Day three
- Test yourself to perfection on all the **New words**.
- Read and learn the **Good news grammar**.

Day four (the tough day)
- Cut out and learn the **Flash sentences**.
- Listen to/Read **Learn by heart**.

Day five
- Listen to/Read **Let's speak Spanish**.
- Go over **Learn by heart**.

Day six
- Listen to/Read **Spot the keys**.
- Listen to/Read **Let's speak more Spanish** (optional).
- Listen to/Read **Let's speak Spanish – fast and fluently** (optional).
- Translate **Test your progress**.

Day seven
How is the Progress chart looking? Great?… Great!

I bet you don't want a day off… but I insist!

On the move

Tom and Kate travel through Castilla – by train, bus and hire car.

(At the railway station)

Tom   Two tickets to Toledo, please.

Clerk   Thereandback?

Tom   There and what? Speak more slowly, please.

Clerk   There – and – back?

Tom   Only single, please. When is there a train for Toledo and on what platform?

Clerk   At a quarter to ten, on platform number six.

Kate   Come on, Tom, there are two seats here in non-smoking. Oh, there is somebody here who smokes*. Excuse me, this is for non-smokers. It is forbidden to smoke here.

Man   Sorry, I don't understand, I speak only English.

(At the bus stop)

Kate   They say that the bus for Madrid is coming in about 20 minutes. Tom, please, here are my postcards and a letter. There is a letter box down there. I am going to take some photos of the river. It is very lovely with the sun.

Tom   Kate, come on, two buses are coming. The two are yellow. This one is full. Let's take the other one. *(In the bus)* Two to Madrid, please.

Driver This bus goes to Toledo.

Tom   But we are in Toledo!

Driver Yes, yes, but this bus goes only to the Toledo hospital.

(In the car)

Tom   Here comes our car. It costs only €40 for three days. I am very pleased.

Kate   I do not like the car. I believe that it is very cheap because it is very old. Let's hope we do not have problems…

* Smoking is no longer permitted in any compartment on Spanish trains

De acá para allá

🔊 CD2, tr 13

Tom and Kate travel through Castilla – by train, bus and hire car.

(En la estación de ferrocarril)

Tom   Dos billetes para Toledo, por favor.

Clerk   ¿Idayvuelta?

Tom   ¿Ida y qué? Hable más despacio, por favor.

Clerk   ¿Ida – y – vuelta?

Tom   Sólo ida, por favor. ¿Cuándo hay un tren para Toledo y en qué vía?

Clerk   A las diez menos cuarto, en la vía número seis.

Kate   Venga, Tom, hay dos asientos aquí en no fumadores. Oh, aquí hay alguien que fuma. Perdone, esto es para no fumadores. Está prohibido fumar aquí.

Man   Sorry, no comprendo. Hablo only English.

(En la parada del autobús)

Kate   Dicen que el autobús para Madrid viene en unos veinte minutos. Tom, por favor, aquí están mis tarjetas y una carta. Allí abajo hay un buzón. Yo voy a hacer unas fotos del río. Está muy bonito con el sol.

Tom   Kate, venga, vienen dos autobuses. Los dos son amarillos. Éste está lleno. Vamos a tomar el otro. (En el autobús) Dos a Madrid, por favor.

Driver Este autobús va a Toledo.

Tom   ¡Pero si estamos en Toledo!

Driver Sí, sí, pero este autobús va sólo al hospital de Toledo.

(En el coche)

Tom   Aquí viene nuestro coche. Cuesta sólo cuarenta euros por tres días. Estoy muy contento.

Kate   El coche no me gusta. Creo que es muy barato porque es muy viejo. Espero no tener problemas…

Tom   I am sorry, but the first car was too expensive, the second one too big, this one was the last.

(Later)

The map is not (here). Where is the motorway? On the left there is a petrol station and a stop for the underground and on the right there is a school. Come on!

Kate   The main road is over there, (where) the traffic light. If we go to the end of the street we arrive at the motorway. Perhaps some three kilometres. (On the motorway) Why does the car go very slowly? Do we have enough petrol? How many litres? Do we have oil? The engine is hot. I believe the car has broken down. Where is the mobile? Where is the number of the garage? Where is my handbag?

Tom   Kate, please, all this is giving me a headache! And here comes the rain. And why are the police driving behind us?

Tom   Lo siento, pero el primer coche era demasiado caro,
el segundo demasiado grande, éste era el último.

(Más tarde)

El mapa no está. ¿Dónde está la autovía? A la izquierda hay
una gasolinera y una parada de metro, y a la derecha hay un
colegio. ¡Venga!

Kate   La carretera está allí, donde el semáforo. Si vamos hasta
el final de la calle llegamos a la autovía. Quizás unos tres
kilómetros. (En la autovía) ¿Por qué va el coche muy lento?
¿Tenemos suficiente gasolina? ¿Cuántos litros? ¿Tenemos
aceite? El motor está caliente. Creo que el coche está roto.
¿Dónde está el movil? ¿Dónde está el número del taller?
¿Dónde está mi bolso?

Tom   Kate, por favor, todo esto me da dolor de cabeza. ¡Y aquí
viene la lluvia! ¿Y por qué va la policía detrás de nosotros?

New words

🔊 CD2, tr 14

de acá para allá from here to there, on the move
la estación the station
el ferrocarril the railway
el billete the ticket
ida y vuelta return ticket ('going and returning')
hable speak
más despacio more slowly
¿cuándo? when?
el tren the train
la vía the platform
venga come!, come on!
no fumadores non-smoking
fuma he/she/it smokes, you smoke
prohibido forbidden
fumar (to) smoke
comprendo I understand
hablo I speak
la parada the stop
el autobus the bus
dicen they say
viene he/she/it comes, you come
las tarjetas the postcards
la carta the letter
abajo below, downstairs
el buzón the letter box
hacer do, make
la foto the photo
el río the river
el sol the sun
vienen they come
éste this one
lleno full
el otro, la otra the other

si if
el hospital the hospital
el coche the car
por for
contento/a pleased
porque because
viejo/a old
espero I hope
el problema the problem
segundo/a second
último/a last
el mapa the map
la autovía the motorway
la gasolinera the petrol station
el metro the underground
un colegio a school, college
la carretera the main road
el semáforo the traffic light
el final the end
la calle the street
llegamos we arrive
el kilómetro the kilometre
¿por qué? why?
lento/a slow
suficiente enough
la gasolina the petrol
el litro the litre
el aceite the oil
el motor the motor
caliente hot
el taller repair garage
me me
da he/she/it gives, you give
el dolor de cabeza the headache
la lluvia the rain
la policía the police

TOTAL NEW WORDS: 69
... only 29 words to go!

Good news grammar

🔊 CD2, tr 15

1 *Lo* and *la:* 'it' – *los* and *las:* 'them'

If you want to refer to something or someone – **el camarero, la cuenta, los servicios** or **las tortillas** – in English, you would say *it* or *them*. In Spanish you use **lo** (for **el** words), **la, los** or **las**. **Tengo el coche.** *I have it.* **Lo tengo. Tengo la cuenta.** *I have it.* **¡La tengo!** Easy! The **lo, la, los** or **las** always go in front of the first verb:

> **Mi marido la (la ducha) puede reparar.**
> *My husband it can repair.*

2 *¿Por qué?... porque...* (twins, but not identical)

Por qué means *why?* Think of it as *'for what?'*

Porque means *because*. Think of it as *'for that...'*

3 *¿Qué?... que...* 'what?'... 'that'... (more twins, not identical)

Have you noticed that all the question words carry accents?

> **¿cuándo? ¿cuánto? ¿cómo? ¿dónde? ¿qué?**
> *when? how much? how? where? what?*

Some of these reappear without the accent to introduce the answer.

> **¿Cómo es Bombay?** *How is Bombay?*
> **Como Nueva York.** *Like New York.*

> **¿Cuándo trabaja usted?** *When do you work?*
> **Cuando me gusta.** *When I like to.*

4 Pronouns: *me, mí, le, lo, la, él, ella, nos, les, los, las, ellos, ellas...* and more

Learning these 'cold' is a bit difficult. Pick them up from the stories or from the **Flash sentences**. It's easier that way.

Learn by heart

🔊 CD2, tr 16

Someone has crashed the car and someone else is getting suspicious…
Say these lines like a prize-winning play!

Vamos al tenis

A   **¿Vamos al tenis? Tengo dos billetes de la empresa.**
        Me gustan mucho los americanos. Vamos en autobús
        o quizás en el metro. Hay también un tren, todo el día.

B   **¿El autobús, el metro, un tren? ¿Por qué? Hay algo que**
        no me gusta. Tenemos un coche abajo en la calle.

A   **Pues… con la lluvia no he visto el semáforo. Pero no es**
        mucho, sólo la puerta, ¡y el jefe* del taller era muy amable!

*el jefe: *the boss*

Let's speak Spanish

CD2, tr 17

Here's your ten-point warm up: respond to the answers with a question, referring to the words in CAPITAL LETTERS.

Example **PEDRO está aquí. ¿QUIÉN está aquí?**

1 El móvil no está EN MI BOLSO.
2 LA AUTOVÍA está al final de la carretera.
3 Hay un autobús EN VEINTE MINUTOS.
4 MI MARIDO quisiera hablar con el Señor González.
5 Ida y vuelta a Madrid cuesta QUINCE EUROS.
6 La casa no me gusta PORQUE ES VIEJA.
7 Van a Inglaterra EN COCHE.
8 Habla inglés MUY LENTO.
9 NO, el sueldo no me gusta.
10 SÍ, he estado contenta en el colegio.

While out shopping with a friend you are offered various items to buy. You'll take them all saying: *Yes, we'll buy it* or *Yes, we'll buy them*.

11 ¿...y la cerveza?
12 ¿...y el periódico?
13 ¿...y los pollos?
14 ¿...y las camisetas?
15 ¿...y el Mercedes?
16 ¿...y mi casa?

Here are four things you want to refer to but you don't know how to say them in Spanish. Explain them using the words you do know.

17 an au pair
18 kennels
19 a teacher
20 to be broke

Answers

1 ¿Dónde está el móvil?
2 ¿Qué está al final de la carretera?
3 ¿Cuándo hay un autobús?
4 ¿Quién quisiera hablar con el Señor González?
5 ¿Cuánto cuesta a Madrid ida y vuelta?
6 ¿Por qué no le gusta la casa?
7 ¿En qué van a Inglaterra?
8 ¿Cómo habla inglés?
9 ¿Le gusta el sueldo?
10 ¿Ha estado contenta en el colegio?
11 Sí, la compramos.
12 Sí, lo compramos.
13 Sí, los compramos.
14 Sí, las compramos.
15 ¡Sí, lo compramos!
16 ¡Sí, la compramos!
17 Una señora que ayuda con el trabajo en la casa.
18 Una casa para los perros cuando estamos de vacaciones.
19 Una señora o un señor que trabaja con los niños en el colegio.
20 No tenemos dinero.

Let's speak more Spanish

🔊 CD2, tr 18

In your own words

This exercise will teach you to express yourself freely. Use only the words you have learned so far.

Tell me in your own words that…

1 you bought a return ticket to Almería
2 you believe there is a train at 10.15
3 you have a seat in non-smoking
4 on Monday you wouldn't mind going by bus to Toledo
5 you must take some photos for your company.
6 this bus is crowded; you are going to take the other one
7 your car is coming on Thursday; it is new but very cheap
8 your wife says 'It's terrible, I don't like it'
9 she says the car is too slow and the engine always overheats
10 hopefully you won't have problems

Answers

1 **He comprado un billete de ida y vuelta para Almería.**
2 **Creo que hay un tren a las diez y cuarto.**
3 **Tengo un asiento en no fumadores.**
4 **El lunes quisiera ir a Toledo en autobús.**
5 **Tengo que tomar unas fotos para mi empresa.**
6 **Este autobús está lleno. Voy a tomar el otro.**
7 **Mi coche viene el jueves. Es nuevo pero muy barato.**
8 **Mi mujer dice: 'Es terrible, no me gusta.'**
9 **Dice que el coche es demasiado lento y el motor está siempre muy caliente.**
10 **Espero no tener problemas.**

Let's speak Spanish – fast and fluently

🔊 CD2, tr 19

Translate each section and check if it is correct, then cover up the answers and say the three or four sentences fast!

A ticket to Madrid, please. Only one way.
How much? I am sorry, please speak more slowly.
Yes, I would like a seat – one way only.

Un billete para Madrid por favor, sólo ida.
¿Cuánto? Lo siento, hable más despacio, por favor.
Sí, quisiera un asiento – sólo ida.

My wife is going to take a photo of the letter box.
In Spain the letter boxes are yellow, not red like in England.
Unfortunately, it is full.
What are we going to do with the letters?

Mi mujer va a tomar una foto del buzón.
En España, los buzones son amarillos, no rojos como en Inglaterra.
Desgraciadamente, está lleno.
¿Qué hacemos con las cartas?

We don't have a map of Andalucía.
I can't see the road to the motorway.
All the traffic lights are (in) red.
My wife has a headache.
Oh dear.

No tenemos un mapa de Andalucía.
No puedo ver la carretera a la autovía.
Todos los semáforos están en rojo.
Mi mujer tiene dolor de cabeza.
¡Madre mía!

Spot the keys

🔊 CD2, tr 20

This time you plan a trip in the country and wonder about the weather. This is what you would ask:

You   Perdone, ¿sabe qué tiempo tenemos hoy?

Answer *Pues,* no estoy *muy* segura, pero *de acuerdo con la última previsión* en la tele *hay un sistema lento de bajas presiones que se está alejando hacia el norte y se espera que* hoy *el* tiempo *sea bastante* caliente, *es decir unos* treinta *grados, pero por la* noche *se espera algunas tormentas y* lluvia.

She isn't sure, but according to the TV, something slow is happening (?) and it will be warm tomorrow – 30°C – but something (?) and rain in the night.

Test your progress

Translate the following into Spanish.

1 I don't like this car. The other car was better.
2 How much does the ticket cost – one way only?
3 What did you say? Speak more slowly, please.
4 We hope to buy petrol cheaper (more cheap) in Spain.
5 It is forbidden to smoke in the underground.
6 Is this correct? A yellow letter box? I did not know it.
7 Can I speak with the mechanic? We are (at) 30 km from Madrid.
8 What is slower: the train or the car on (in) the motorway?
9 He did not see the traffic light, and now they are in the hospital.
10 There is a chemist's on (in) the main road, at (in) the bus stop.
11 I would like two return tickets, non-smoking.
12 The problem with her is that she smokes too much.
13 He has come here, to the end of the platform.
14 There is a lot of rain in England. I am pleased to be in Spain.
15 They say that the river is five minutes from the station.
16 If he does not give me the money, I am going to the police.
17 This is the last petrol station. Do we have enough oil and water?
18 They come in July. I do not understand why Pedro comes later.
19 I speak with him now. I have a mobile.
20 He has not eaten anything because he has (a) headache.

If you know all your words you should score over 90%!

Week 6

Day-by-day guide

This is your last week! Need I say more?

Day one

- Read **In the airport**.
- Listen to/Read **En el aeropuerto**.
- Read the **New words**. There are only 29!

Day two

- Repeat **En el aeropuerto**. Learn all the **New words**.
- Work with the **Flash words** and **Flash sentences**.

Day three

- Test yourself on the **Flash sentences**.
- Listen to/Read and learn **¡Adiós!**

Day four

- No more **Good news grammar**! Have a look at the summary.
- Read **Say it simply**.

Day five

- Listen to/Read **Spot the keys**.
- Listen to/Read **Let's speak Spanish**.

Day six

- Listen to/Read **Let's speak more Spanish** (optional).
- Listen to/Read **Let's speak Spanish – fast and fluently** (optional).
- Your last **Test your progress!** Go for it!

Day seven

> **Congratulations!**
> **You have successfully completed the course**
> **and can now speak**
> ***Fast Spanish with Elisabeth Smith!***

In the airport

It's the end of the trip and time to go home. There's one more surprise for Tom and Kate when they bump into an old friend in the departure lounge.

Tom　　We have to work on Monday. What a bore. I would like to go to Italy, or better, to Hawaii. My company can wait and nobody is going to know where I am.

Kate　　And what are the people in my company going to say? They are going to wait for two days and then they are going to phone my mother. She certainly knows the number of my mobile. And then?

Tom　　Yes, yes, I know (it). Well, perhaps a week's holiday at Christmas in the snow or on a boat to Madeira... I am going to buy a newspaper... Kate, here is Pedro Iglesias!

Pedro　　Well, hello! How are you? What are you doing here? This is my wife, Nancy. How were your holidays? Are they finished?

Kate　　The holidays...? hmmm... great. Now we know Andalucia and Castilla well.

Pedro　　Next year you must go to Santander or Pamplona. Mrs Walker, my wife would like to buy a book about computers. Would you mind going with her and helping her, please? Mr Walker, you have a newspaper. What is happening with the football? And... would you like to have a drink?

(In a shop at the airport)

Kate　　I don't see anything. There is nothing that I like. Are you also going to England?

Nancy　　No, we are going to Madrid to (the house of) Pedro's mother. Our children are always there during the holidays. We have one son and three daughters. Tomorrow we are going to take the train. It is cheaper.

Kate　　Your husband works for the Bank of Spain, doesn't he?

Nancy　　Yes, his work is interesting but the pay is bad. We have a small apartment and an old car. We have to repair lots of things. My mother is in Los Angeles and I have a girlfriend in Dallas and we write (to us) a lot of e-mails. I would like to go to America but it costs too much money.

78 Kate　　But you have a lovely house in Mallorca.

En el aeropuerto

🔊 CD2, tr 21

It's the end of the trip and time to go home. There's one more surprise for Tom and Kate when they bump into an old friend in the departure lounge.

Tom   El lunes tenemos que trabajar. Qué lata. Quisiera ir a Italia o mejor a Hawaii. Mi empresa puede esperar, y nadie va a saber dónde estoy.

Kate   ¿Y qué va a decir la gente en mi empresa? Van a esperar durante dos días y después van a llamar a mi madre. Seguro que ella sabe el número de mi móvil. ¿Y después?

Tom   Sí, sí, lo sé. Pues, quizás en Navidad una semana de vacaciones en la nieve o en barco a Madeira… Voy a comprar el periódico… Kate, ¡aquí está Pedro Iglesias!

Pedro   ¡Hombre! ¿Qué tal?¿Qué hacen aquí? Ésta es mi mujer, Nancy. ¿Qué tal las vacaciones, han terminado?

Kate   ¿Las vacaciones…? hmmm… estupendas. Ahora conocemos bien Andalucía y Castilla.

Pedro   El año que viene tienen que ir a Santander o Pamplona. Señora Walker, mi mujer quisiera comprar un libro de ordenadores. ¿Le importaría ir con ella y ayudarla, por favor? Señor Walker, usted tiene un periódico. ¿Qué pasa con el fútbol? Y…¿quiere tomar una copa?

(En una tienda del aeropuerto)

Kate   No veo nada. No hay nada que me gusta. ¿Va usted también a Inglaterra?

Nancy   No, vamos a Madrid a casa de la madre de Pedro. Nuestros niños siempre están allí durante las vacaciones. Tenemos un hijo y tres hijas. Mañana vamos a tomar el tren. Es más barato.

Kate   Su marido trabaja en el Banco de España, ¿verdad?

Nancy   Sí, su trabajo es interesante, pero el sueldo es malo. Tenemos un piso pequeño y un coche viejo. Tenemos que reparar muchas cosas. Mi madre está en Los Ángeles y tengo una amiga en Dallas y nos escribimos muchos correos electrónicos. Quisiera ir a América pero cuesta demasiado dinero.

Kate   Pero usted tiene una casa bonita en Mallorca.

79

Nancy   A house in Mallorca? I have never been in Mallorca. When we have holidays we go to (the house of) a friend in Bilbao.

Tom   Kate, come on, we have to go to the plane. Goodbye… What is the matter, Kate? What did Nancy say?

Kate   Wait Tom, wait…

Nancy ¿Una casa en Mallorca? No he estado nunca en Mallorca. Cuando tenemos vacaciones vamos a la casa de un amigo en Bilbao.

Tom Kate, venga, tenemos que ir al avión. Adiós…¿Qué pasa, Kate? ¿Qué ha dicho Nancy?

Kate Espera, Tom, espera…

New words

🔊 CD2, tr 22

el aeropuerto the airport
¡qué lata! what a bore, nuisance!
esperar (to) wait
saber (to) know (a fact)
decir (to) say
la gente the people
llamar (por teléfono) (to) call (on the phone)
la madre the mother
sé I know
en Navidad at Christmas
la nieve the snow
el barco the ship, boat
¡hombre! well, hello! (surprise greeting)
hacen they do, you do
conocemos we know

el libro the book
¿Le importaría? Would you mind?
¿qué pasa? what is happening? what is the matter?
una copa a drink
veo I see
el hijo the son, child (m.)
la hija the daughter, child (f.)
el piso the apartment, flat
vive he/she/it lives, you live
nos us
escribimos we write
el correo electrónico the e-mail
espera/espere wait (friendly)/ (formal)
nunca never

> **TOTAL NEW WORDS: 29**
> **Total SPANISH words learned: 393**
> **Extra words: 78**
> **GRAND TOTAL: 471**

Learn by heart

🔊 CD2, tr 23

This is your last dialogue to learn by heart. Give it your best! You now have a large store of everyday sayings which will be very useful.

> **¡Adiós…!**
>
> **Kate** Señor Gálvez, buenos días, soy Kate Walker. Llamo del aeropuerto. Sí, las vacaciones han terminado y el dinero también, desgraciadamente. Tom quisiera hablar con usted… y…¡adiós!
>
> **Tom** ¡Hola, Juan! ¿Qué? ¿Cómo? ¿Compra los dos? ¿Mi empresa tiene su correo electrónico? ¡Estupendo! ¡Muchas gracias! ¿El año que viene? Kate quisiera ir a Italia, pero a mí me gusta España. ¿Con Edith Palmer? ¡Por favor! Tenemos que ir al avión…¡Adiós!

Good news grammar

As promised there is no new grammar in this lesson, just a summary of all the 31 verbs which appear in the six weeks.

Basic form	I	You, he, she, it	We	They, you	The past: *haber +...*
ayudar*	ayudo	ayuda	ayudamos	ayudan	ayudado
beber*	bebo	bebe	bebemos	beben	bebido
comer*	como	come	comemos	comen	comido
comprar*	compro	compra	compramos	compran	comprado
comprender*	comprendo	comprende	comprendemos	comprenden	comprendido
conocer	conozco	conoce	conocemos	conocen	conocido
creer*	creo	cree	creemos	creen	creido
costar		cuesta		cuestan	
dar	doy	da	damos	dan	dado
decir	digo	dice	decimos	dicen	dicho
escribir	escribo	escribe	escribimos	escriben	escrito
esperar*	espero	espera	esperamos	esperan	esperado
estar	estoy	está	estamos	están	estado
fumar*	fumo	fuma	fumamos	fuman	fumado
haber	he	ha	hemos	han	
hablar*	hablo	habla	hablamos	hablan	hablado
hacer	hago	hace	hacemos	hacen	hecho
ir	voy	va	vamos	van	ido
llamar*	llamo	llama	llamamos	llaman	llamado
llegar*	llego	llega	llegamos	llegan	llegado
poder	puedo	puede	podemos	pueden	podido
querer	quisiera	quisiera	quisiéramos	quisieran	
reparar*	reparo	repara	reparamos	reparan	reparado
saber	sé	sabe	sabemos	saben	sabido
ser	soy	es	somos	son	sido
tener	tengo	tiene	tenemos	tienen	tenido
tomar*	tomo	toma	tomamos	toman	tomado
trabajar*	trabajo	trabaja	trabajamos	trabajan	trabajado
venir	vengo	viene	venimos	vienen	venido
ver	veo	ve	vemos	ven	visto
vivir	vivo	vive	vivimos	viven	vivido

*member of the Good Verbs Group

Say it simply

Here are two more exercises to practise using simple language:

1 You have just hired a car and notice a big scratch on the left, behind the door. You want to report it so as not to get the bill for it later.

2 You are Kate Walker at the airport, about to catch your flight home when you realize that you have left some clothes behind in the room of your hotel. You phone the hotel to ask the housekeeper to send the things on to you.

What would you say? Say it, then write it down. Then take a look at our examples in the **Answers** section.

Spot the keys

◀ CD2, tr 24

Here are two final practice rounds. If you have the recording, close the book now. Find the key words and try to get the gist of it. Then look at the translation in the **Answers** section.

1 This is what you might ask of a taxi driver:

You   ¿En cuánto tiempo se llega* al aeropuerto y cuánto cuesta?

Answer *Depende de la hora en que vaya a salir. Normalmente se llega en unos veinte minutos, pero si viajamos en hora punta y hay mucho tráfico y si hay atascos sobre el puente del río debe calcular unos cuarenta y cinco minutos. El precio se indica en el taxímetro. Normalmente cuesta entre veinte y veinticinco euros.*

(*in how much time does one arrive = how long does it take)

2 While killing time in the departure lounge of the airport you can't help listening to someone who seems to be raving about something. Identify keys and guess where they have been:

… y mi marido dijo también que le había gustado mucho más que nuestras vacaciones aquí. Y la gente era muy amable y no tan reservada como siempre dicen. Y el hotel estaba directamente sobre el lago, con unas habitaciones muy bonitas y hacía un tiempo estupendo y paseámos muchísimo y también fuimos de excursión con el coche y vimos tantas cosas interesantes. Y entonces decidimos sin más que el año que viene vamos a volver…

Let's speak Spanish

🔊 CD2, tr 25

Answer these questions using the words in brackets.

1 ¿Ha comprado el piso en Marbella? (Sí, lo, lunes)
2 ¿Cuántos años ha trabajado allí? (durante tres)
3 ¿Cuándo ha hablado con la empresa? (con ella, esta semana)
4 ¿Por qué tiene que reparar su coche? (mi coche, porque es viejo)
5 ¿Ha ido primero con su madre? (no, con el cliente)

Now say each sentence out loud, translating the English words into Spanish.

6 Alguien ha dicho que está loco (*if you buy this old flat*).
7 Alguien ha dicho que no le gusta (*if we eat too late*).
8 Ha dicho que algo está roto (*if you have no hot water*).
9 Mi amiga ha dicho (*that our holidays are over*).
10 Ha dicho también (*that next year we go to America*).
11 Mi mujer quisiera decir (*that she has a cold*).
12 Mi marido dice que no puede venir (*because he works on a ship*).
13 No puede venir en Navidad (*because his friend is coming*).
14 Mi amigo dice (*that you are very good-looking*).
15 También dice (*that he would like your (su) mobile number*).

Answers

1 Sí, lo he comprado el lunes.
2 He trabajado allí durante tres años.
3 He hablado con ella esta semana.
4 Tengo que reparar mi coche porque es viejo.
5 No, primero he ido con el cliente.
6 ...si compra este piso viejo.
7 ...si comemos demasiado tarde.
8 ...si no tiene agua caliente.
9 ...que nuestras vacaciones han terminado.
10 ...que el año que viene vamos a América.
11 ...que tiene un resfriado.
12 ...porque trabaja en un barco.
13 ...porque viene su amigo.
14 ...que usted es muy guapo/a.
15 ...que quisiera su número móvil.

Let's speak more Spanish

◀) CD2, tr 26

In your own words

This exercise will teach you to express yourself freely. Use only the words you have learned so far.

Tell me in your own words that...

1 next week you have to work
2 you don't like it; you'd rather have more leave
3 nobody knows that you are in Italy
4 your mother has the number of your mobile phone
5 your vacation in Spain was wonderful
6 you did a lot of sightseeing and overeating
7 your friend Mr López is on his way to Granada today
8 he is catching a train to Seville tomorrow
9 you and your wife must fly to America, because your father is ill.
10 you would like to go to Africa for Christmas, but by boat.

Answers

1 **La semana que viene tengo que trabajar.**
2 **No me gusta. Quisiera tener más vacaciones.**
3 **Nadie sabe que estoy en Italia.**
4 **Mi madre tiene el número de mi móvil.**
5 **Las vacaciones en España eran estupendas.**
6 **He visto mucho y he comido más.**
7 **Mi amigo, el señor López, va hoy a Granada.**
8 **Va a tomar el tren para Sevilla mañana.**
9 **Mi mujer y yo tenemos que ir a América porque mi padre está enfermo.**

10 **Quisiera ir a África en Navidad, pero en barco.**

Let's speak Spanish – fast and fluently

🔊 CD2, tr 27

Translate each section and check if it is correct, then cover up the answers and say the three or four sentences fast!

If you manage to say each section in less than 20 seconds give yourself a pat on the back.

The people in my company do not work a lot.
They write many letters on the computer and always talk on the mobile phone.

La gente en mi empresa no trabaja mucho.
Escriben muchas cartas en el ordenador y siempre hablan por el móvil.

I know Andalucía and Castilla very well.
Next year I would like to see Santander.
I must buy a book of the Paradors of Spain.

Conozco muy bien Andalucía y Castilla.
Quisiera ver Santander el año que viene.
Tengo que comprar un libro de los paradores de España.

Well, hello, what are you doing here? What's the matter?
I need to repair my car and my flat. Both (the two) are very old.
The bill is terrible. Can you help me please – with 200 euros?

Hombre, ¿qué hace aquí? ¿Qué pasa?
Tengo que reparar mi coche y mi piso. Los dos son muy viejos.
La cuenta es terrible. ¿Puede ayudarme, por favor – con doscientos euros?

Now say all the sentences in Spanish without stopping and starting.

Test your progress

A lot has been included in this last test – including all 31 verbs!

But don't panic – it looks worse than it is. Go for it – you'll do brilliantly!

Translate into Spanish.

1 I like writing letters because I have a new computer.
2 How are you? What is the matter? Can I help you?
3 The people in the company are (is) rather boring.
4 I do not have the number of her mobile, I am sorry.
5 Do you like the Sierra Nevada? We had a lot of snow this year.
6 The second case is in the bus. Did you see the black bag?
7 How many cards did you write (at) (in) Christmas? Eighty-eight?
8 That's terrible. They have not eaten for five days.
9 Why did you not telephone? We waited since yesterday.
10 When we arrive we'll have (we take) a drink – or two.
11 Don't you know that? The airport is always open – day and night.
12 We are sure that he has done it.
13 We have worked (for) many years but never on a boat.
14 I have given my car to my son. He is very pleased.
15 Your mother is very nice and makes great paella.
16 Do you live in a house or a flat in Torremolinos?
17 We must work many hours. Four daughters cost a lot of money.
18 Can the garage repair that? I hope so.
19 I know him. He always goes shopping with his dog.
20 Who said one cannot smoke here?
21 We go by plane to Dallas. Then we go by car to Las Vegas.
22 I would like to speak with the sales assistant. He did not give me the bill.
23 We drank your wine but we have come today with two more bottles.
24 I am sorry, but **Fast Spanish with Elisabeth Smith** is now finished.

Check your answers then enter a final excellent score on the **Progress chart** and write out your **Certificate**.

Answers

How to score

From a total of 100%

- Subtract 1% for each wrong or missing word.
- Subtract 1% for the wrong form of the verb. For example, we have **tengo** (**tenemos**).
- Subtract 1% every time you mix up the present and the past tenses.

There are no penalties for:

- wrong use of all those little words, like: **el/la**, **un/una**, etc.
- wrong ending of adjectives like: **un coche barata** (**barato**).
- wrong use of **ser** and **estar**
- wrong choice of words with similar meaning like **en** and **a**
- wrong or different word order
- wrong spelling or missing accents – as long as you can say the word: **qué/que**, **quatro** (**cuatro**), **ora** (**hora**), **rotto** (**roto**), etc.
- missing or incorrect punctuation like ¿ or ¡.

> **100% MINUS YOUR PENALTIES WILL GIVE YOU YOUR WEEKLY SCORE.**

Week 1: Test your progress

1 Me llamo Peter Smith.
2 ¡Hola, somos Helen y Pepe!
3 Soy de Toledo. ¿Y usted?
4 María es una buena amiga.
5 Siempre voy a casa en junio.
6 Trabajamos en Alicante en agosto.
7 ¿(Usted) Va siempre a Nueva York en marzo?
8 ¿En qué trabaja (usted)? ¿Trabaja (usted) con ordenadores?
9 Está en Londres con los niños.
10 Un momento por favor. ¿Qué es? ¿Cuesta mucho?
11 ¿La casa tiene teléfono? No, desgraciadamente, no.
12 Buenos días. ¿Es usted la señora López de Madrid?
13 Trabajo sin sueldo en una empresa americana.
14 Ahora tengo un trabajo mejor. Trabajo para tres bancos grandes.
15 ¡Paco! ¿Qué tal? ¿Vamos a Sevilla?
16 Mi mujer también es americana. Es de Boston.
17 Tenemos buenos asientos en el avión.
18 ¿Yo tengo un Mercedes? ¡Qué va!
19 Mi amiga habla español, pero no mucho.
20 Voy de vacaciones con Carmen. Desgraciadamente es aburrida.

Your score: _____ %

Correct those answers which differ from ours. Then read our versions out loud twice.

Week 2: Test your progress

1 ¿Dónde hay un teléfono? ¿A la derecha?
2 ¿Podemos comer unas tostadas aquí? ¿Hay asientos para cuatro?
3 ¿Tiene una mesa? ¿A las ocho y media? Somos seis.
4 Vamos a la cafetería, ¿vale?
5 ¿Puede reparar el Seat? Está roto.
6 Estamos en la habitación. ¿Dónde está (usted)?
7 Las tapas están estupendas. Puedo comer muchas.
8 ¿Puedo preguntarle? (Usted) Tiene una empresa pequeña.
   ¿Está en Texas?
9 No podemos ir de vacaciones en julio. No tenemos dinero.

10 ¿Dónde está el camarero? ¿Tiene mi cuenta?

11 ¿Dónde están los servicios? ¿A la izquierda?

12 María y yo quisiéramos ir a Granada – sin maridos.

13 Perdone, tengo sólo treinta y cinco euros y una tarjeta de crédito.

14 ¿Tres euros y diez céntimos para una tortilla fría? Es muy cara.

15 He estado en Sevilla para una noche. Cuesta menos en noviembre.

16 La Señora López es muy guapa. ¿Dónde trabaja? ¿Muy cerca?

17 ¡De acuerdo! Tomamos el Seat para abril.

18 Londres no es bonito en noviembre.

19 He trabajado un poco con ordenadores. No es fácil.

20 ¿A qué hora vamos a estar aquí? A la una.

Your score: _____ %

Week 3: Test your progress

1 Podemos comprar sellos en el estanco, ¿verdad?

2 ¿Ha visto el tenis en la tele? Sí, he visto todo.

3 Era muy amable, como siempre.

4 ¡Madre mía! ¡Los huevos están rotos! No importa.

5 Ayer era un día bastante bueno.

6 El periódico inglés no era barato.

7 Creo que he visto una tintorería en El Corte Inglés.

8 ¿Hasta qué hora tiene que trabajar? ¿Hasta las ocho?

9 ¿A qué hora tenemos que ir? No puedo ir hasta más tarde.

10 En noviembre siempre hace mal tiempo en Manchester.

11 ¿Qué ha comprado? ¿Seis botellas de vino tinto? ¡Estupendo!

12 Talla cuarenta y cuatro: ¿qué es eso en inglés? Quizás catorce.

13 Hace mucho frío en esta casa. Tengo que comprar algo.

14 Primero he ido de compras y después hemos comido con amigos.

15 Hemos tenido la nueva tele desde ayer. ¡Y hoy está rota!

16 Ha comprado una maleta negra, no roja ¿verdad?

17 Todo era muy caro. Entonces no hemos comprado nada.

18 ¿Quién es el dependiente? Dónde está la leche?

19 No tenemos la camiseta en verde y al mismo precio.

20 Quisiera comprar algo para mí. Pero no demasiado caro.

Your score: _____ %

Week 4: Test your progress

1 ¿Qué ha dicho? Ha dicho: '¿Para quién son las patatas fritas?'
2 ¿Puede venir a nuestra casa? ¿La semana que viene?
3 Dice que la salida de la tienda está arriba, detrás del bar.
4 ¿Ha dicho que ha ido a Inglaterra?
5 ¿Qué quiere? Es que… estoy enfermo y no puedo trabajar.
6 ¿Podría ayudarme, por favor? ¿Hay un doctor aquí?
7 ¿Va a la cita sin zapatos? Esto no se puede hacer.
8 Conozco a Isabel Romero. Es una señora muy interesante.
9 Nadie puede beber quince cervezas en una noche. No es posible.
10 El postre me gusta mucho. Quisiera el helado.
11 Dice que es una cosa importante pero no tiene tiempo.
12 Hemos terminado y ahora tenemos que ir a Valencia.
13 Como muchas ensaladas. ¿Qué come usted?
14 ¿Cómo le gusta el pescado? ¿Sin ajo?
15 El nombre de esta verdura: ¿cómo se dice… en español?
16 No hay tiendas delante de la iglesia o detrás. ¿Qué hacemos?
17 Ha llamado la empresa. Un Señor López ha dicho que es una cosa importante.
18 Estoy seguro de que tienen agua con gas. La tienen siempre.
19 Dice que tiene dolores desde ayer. ¿Lo cree?
20 Tengo un resfriado. No puedo ir a Inglaterra hoy.

Your score: _____%

Week 5: Test your progress

1 Este coche no me gusta. El otro coche era mejor.
2 ¿Cuánto es/cuesta el billete – sólo ida?
3 ¿Qué ha dicho? Hable más despacio, por favor.
4 Esperamos comprar la gasolina más barata en España.
5 Está prohibido fumar en el metro.
6 ¿Es esto correcto? ¿Un buzón amarillo? No lo he sabido.
7 ¿Puedo hablar con el taller? Estamos a treinta kilómetros de Madrid.
8 ¿Qué es más lento? ¿El tren o el coche en la autovía?
9 No ha visto el semáforo, y ahora están en el hospital.
10 Hay una farmacia en la carretera, en la parada de autobús.
11 Quisiera dos billetes de ida y vuelta, no fumadores.
12 El problema con ella es que fuma demasiado.

13 Ha venido aquí, al final de la vía.

14 Hay mucha lluvia en Inglaterra. Estoy contento de estar en España.

15 Dicen que el río está a cinco minutos de la estación.

16 Si no me da el dinero voy a la policía.

17 Esta es la última gasolinera. ¿Tenemos suficiente agua y aceite?

18 Vienen en julio. No comprendo por qué Pedro viene más tarde.

19 Hablo con él ahora. Tengo un móvil.

20 No ha comido nada porque tiene dolor de cabeza.

> Your score: _____%

Week 6: Test your progress

1 Me gusta escribir cartas, porque tengo un nuevo ordenador.

2 ¿Qué tal? ¿Qué pasa? ¿Puedo ayudarle?

3 La gente en la empresa es bastante aburrida.

4 No tengo el número de su móvil, lo siento.

5 ¿Le gusta la Sierra Nevada? Este año hemos tenido mucha nieve.

6 La segunda maleta está en el autobús. ¿Ha visto el bolso negro?

7 ¿Cuántas tarjetas ha escrito en Navidad? ¿Ochenta y ocho?

8 Esto es terrible. No han comido durante cinco días.

9 ¿Por qué no ha llamado por teléfono? Hemos esperado desde ayer.

10 Cuando lleguemos tomamos una copa – o dos.

11 ¿No lo sabe? El aeropuerto está abierto siempre – día y noche.

12 Estamos seguros de que lo ha hecho.

13 Hemos trabajado muchos años pero nunca en un barco.

14 He dado mi coche a mi hijo. Está muy contento.

15 Su madre es muy amable y hace una paella estupenda.

16 ¿Vive usted en un piso o en una casa en Torremolinos?

17 Tenemos que trabajar muchas horas. Cuatro hijas cuestan mucho.

18 ¿Lo puede reparar el taller? Espero que sí.

19 Lo conozco. Siempre va de compras con su perro.

20 ¿Quién ha dicho que no se puede fumar aquí?

21 Vamos a Dallas en avión. Luego vamos a Las Vegas en coche.

22 Quisiera hablar con el dependiente. No me ha dado la cuenta.

23 Hemos bebido su vino pero hemos venido hoy con dos botellas más.

24 Lo siento, pero **Fast Spanish with Elisabeth Smith** ha terminado ahora.

> Your score: _____%

Week 6: Say it simply

1 Perdone, hay un problema con el coche. ¿Puede venir, por favor? Esto, detrás de la puerta, aquí a la izquierda. Yo no lo he hecho. No quisiera tener un problema más tarde.

2 Hola, buenos días, soy Kate Walker. El número de mi habitación es el 32. Llamo del aeropuerto. Tengo unas cosas en la habitación y ahora vamos a Birmingham. Lo siento, pero ¿puede ayudarme por favor? Tengo que tener las cosas. El hotel sabe dónde vivo en Birmingham. Muchas gracias.

Week 6: Spot the keys

1 It depends on the time you are going to leave. Normally it takes about 20 minutes but if we leave in the rush hour and there is a lot of traffic and a traffic jam on the bridge over the river, you have to calculate some 45 or 50 minutes. The price is shown on the meter. Normally it costs between €20 and €25.

2 They have of course been in England!

Spanish–English dictionary

In this section you'll find all the **New words** that you have learned, including the 'extras', in alphabetical order.

To make it easy for you to find what you may have forgotten, words are shown exactly as they appear in the **New words** section. For example, if you learned *a lot* you'll find it under *'a'*. If you don't remember how to say *I work* you'll find it under *'I'*. The only exceptions to this are the nouns. We've put the article, e.g *the* or **el** following the noun. So you'll find *the money* under *'m'* and **el tren** under **'t'**.

a, al to, to the
abajo below, downstairs
abierto open
abril April
aburrido/a boring
aceite, el the oil
adiós goodbye, for longer absence
aeropuerto, el the airport
agosto august
agua (f.), el the water
ahora now
ajo, el the garlic
algo something
alguien someone
allí there
amable kind, charming
amarillo/a yellow
americano/a American
amiga, una a girlfriend
año, el/años, los the year/the years
aquí here
arriba above, upstairs

asientos, los the seats
autobús, el the bus
autovía, la the motorway
avión, el the aeroplane
ayer yesterday
azúcar, el the sugar
azul blue

Banco de España, el the Bank of Spain
barato/a cheap
barco, el the ship, boat
bastante enough, rather
beber (to) drink
bien well, all right
billete, el the ticket
blanco/a white
bolsa, la/bolso, el the bag/ the handbag
bonito/a pretty, lovely, nice
botella, una a bottle
buenas noches good night
buenas tardes good afternoon
bueno/a good

buenos días good day, good morning
buzón, el the letter box

café coffee
cafetería, una a café
cajero (automático), un a cashpoint machine
caliente hot
calle, la the street
camarero, el the waiter
camiseta, la the T-shirt
carne, la the meat
caro/a expensive
carretera, la the main road
carta, la the letter
casa, una/en casa a house/ at home
céntimo, el the cent
centro, al centro centre, to the centre
cerca near
cero zero
cerveza, la the beer
chuletas, las the chops
cien a hundred
cinco five
cita, una an appointment
cliente, el the client
coche, el the car
colegio, un a school, college
colores, los the colours
comer (to) eat
como like, as
cómo… ? how… ?
¿cómo se dice en español…? how does one say in Spanish… ?
comprar (to) buy
comprendo I understand
98 con with

con/sin gas carbonated/ non-carbonated
conocemos we know
conozco (a) I know (usually somebody or a place)
contento/a pleased
copa, una a drink
cordero, el the lamb
correcto correct
correo electrónico, el the e-mail
correos the post office
Corte Inglés, El a Spanish chain of department stores
cosa, una a thing, a matter
creo I believe
¿cuándo? when?
¿cuánto? how much…?
cuarto quarter
cuarto de baño, el the bathroom
cuatro four
cuenta, la the bill
cuesta/cuestan it costs/ they cost

da he/she/it gives, you give
de/del from, of/from, of the
de acá para allá from here to there, on the move
de acuerdo agreed, OK, all right, right
de vacaciones on holiday(s)
decir (to) say
delante (de) in front of
demasiado too, too much
dependiente, el the sales assistant
derecha, a la derecha right, on the right
desayuno, el the breakfast
desde since

desgraciadamente unfortunately
después afterwards, then
detrás (de) behind
días de la semana, los days of the week
dice he/she/it says, you say
dicen they say
diciembre December
diez ten
dinero, el the money
doctor, el the doctor
dolor, el the pain, ache
dolor de cabeza, el the headache
domingo Sunday
¿dónde? where?
dos two
ducha, la the shower
durante during, for

él he, him
el, la, los, las the
ella she, her
empresa, la the company
en in/on
en Navidad at Christmas
enero January
enfermo sick, ill
ensalada, una a salad
entonces and so
era he/she/it was, I was
eran they were
es you are, he/she/it is
es que... it is that, that's because...
escribimos we write
ese, esa/eso (by itself) that
esnob snob, snobbish
espera/espere wait (friendly)/ wait (formal)
esperar (to) wait

espero I hope
está he/she/it is, you are
estación, la the station
están they are, you are (plural)
estanco, el the tobacconist
éste this one
este, esta/esto (by itself) this
estupendo/a marvellous, great

fácil easy
farmacia, la the chemist's
febrero February
ferrocarril, el the railway
filete, un a fillet steak
final, el the end
foto, la the photo
frío/a cold
fruta, la the fruit
fuma he/she/it smokes, you smoke
fumar (to) smoke
fútbol, el the football

gasolina, la the petrol
gasolinera, la the petrol station
gente, la the people
gracias, muchas gracias thank you, thank you very much
gramo, un a gram
grande big
gris grey
guapo/a good looking
gusta, le gusta, me gusta/no me gusta like/you like, do you like? I like (it)/I do not like (it)

ha dicho has said
ha llamado has called
habitación doble, una a double room
habla he/she/it speaks, you speak

99

¡hable! speak!
hablo I speak
hace frío it is cold (it makes cold)
hace mal tiempo it is bad weather (lit. it makes…)
hacemos we do
hacen they do, you do
hacer do, make
hasta until
hasta luego bye, until later
hay there is
he comprado I have bought, I bought
he estado I have been, I was
he ido I have gone
he trabajado I have worked
he visto I have seen
helado ice cream
hemos comido we have eaten
hemos estado we have been, we were
hija, la the daughter, child (f.)
hijo, el the son, child (m.)
hola hello
¡hombre! well, hello! (surprise greeting)
hospital, el the hospital
hoy today
huevos, los the eggs

ida y vuelta return ticket ('going and returning')
iglesia, la the church
importante important
Inglaterra England
inglés English
interesante interesting
ir (to) go
ir de compras go shopping
izquierda, a la izquierda left, on the left

jamón, el the ham
jueves Thursday
julio July
junio June

kilómetro, el the kilometre

la, los, las the
¿Le importaría? would you mind?
leche, la the milk
lento/a slow
libro, el the book
limpio/a clean
litro, el the litre
llamar (por teléfono) (to) call (on the phone)
llegamos we arrive
lleno full
lluvia, la the rain
lo, la (by itself) it
lo siento I'm sorry
loco/a crazy
los the
luego then, later
lunes Monday

¡Madre mía! good grief! (lit. my mother!)
imadre, la the mother
maleta, una suitcase
malo/a bad
mañana tomorrow
mantequilla, la the butter
mapa, el the map
marido, el the husband
marrón brown
martes Tuesday
marzo March
más more
más despacio more slowly
más tarde later

100

mayo May
me me
me llamo... my name is…
medio half
mejor better
menos less
menú, el the menu
mesa, la the table
meses, los the months
metro, el the underground
mi my
miércoles Wednesday
minutos minutes
mismo, el the same
momento, un a moment
motor, el the motor
mucho/a much, a lot
mujer, la the woman, wife
muy very

nada nothing
nadie nobody
naranja orange
negro/a black
nieve, la the snow
niños, los the children
no no, not
no fumadores non-smoking
no importa it doesn't matter,
  no problem
no se puede hacer one cannot
  do that
noche, una a night
nombre, el the name
nos us
nosotros we
noviembre November
nuestro/a our
nueve nine
nuevo/a new
números, los the numbers
nunca never

o or
ocho eight
octubre October
ordenador/es computer/s
otro/a, el/la the other

pan, el the bread
papel, el the paper
para for
para mí for me
parada, la the stop
patatas fritas, las the chips
peluquería, la the hairdresser's
pequeño/a small
perdón excuse me
periódico, un a newspaper
pero but
perro, un a dog
pescado, el the fish
piso, el the apartment, flat
poco, un a little
podemos we can
¿podría ayudarme? could you
  help me?
policia, la the police
pollo asado, el the roast chicken
por for
por favor please
¿por qué? why?
por teléfono on the telephone
porque because
posible possible
postre, el the dessert
precio, el the price
preguntar to ask
primero first
problema, el the problem
prohibido forbidden
puede he/she can, you can
puedo I can
¿puedo preguntarle? Can I ask
  you?

puerta, la the door
pues… well…, well then

que that, as
qué what
¿qué desean? what do you want/wish?
¡qué lata! what a bore, nuisance!
¿qué pasa? what is happening?, what is the matter?
¿qué quiere? what do you want?
¿qué tal? how are you, how is…?
¿qué tienen ustedes? What do you have?
¡qué va! come off it!
queso, el the cheese
¿quién? who?
quisiera/quisiéramos I/we would like (to)
quizás perhaps

reparar (to) repair
resfriado, un a cold
restaurante, el the restaurant
río, el the river
rojo/a red
rosa pink
roto/a broken, broken down

sábado Saturday
saber (to) know (a fact)
salida, la the exit
sé I know
segundo/a second
seguro (de) sure (about)
seis six
sellos, los the stamps
102 semáforo, el the traffic light

semana que viene, la next week (the week that comes)
señora Mrs, woman
septiembre September
servicios, los the toilets
si if
sí yes
siempre always
siete seven
sin without
sol, el the sun
sólo only
somos we are
son are, they are
sopa, una a soup
soy I am
sueldo, el the pay, salary
suficiente enough
supermercado, un a supermarket

talla, la the size
taller, el repair garage
también also
tapas Spanish snacks
tarjetas, las the postcards
tarjetas de crédito, las the credit cards
té, un a tea
tele, televisión, la the TV
teléfono móvil, el the mobile (phone)
tenemos we have
tenemos que we have to, we must
tengo I have
tengo que I have to, must
terminado finished
terrible terrible
tiempo time, also: weather
tienda, la the shop
tiene he/she/it has, you have

tintorería, la the dry cleaner's
todo all
todo recto straight ahead
tomamos we take
tomar (to) take
tortilla, una a Spanish omelette
tostadas toast
trabaja he/she/it works,
   you work
trabajamos we work
trabajo I work, also: (the) work
treinta metros thirty metres
treinta y cinco thirty five
tren, el the train
tres three

último/a last
un, una a, one
uno one
unos, unas some
usted/ustedes you (one person)/
   you (more than one person)

va he/she/it goes, you go
vale all right, OK

vamos we go, we are going,
   let's go!
vaso, un a glass
venga come!, come on!
venir (to) come
veo I see
¿verdad? isn't it, aren't they,
   don't you, etc.
verde green
verdura, la the vegetables
via, la the platform
viejo/a old
viene he/she/it comes,
   you come
vienen they come
viernes Friday
vino tinto, el the red wine
vive he/she/it lives,
   you live
voy I go, I am going

y and
yo I

zapatos, los the shoes

English–Spanish dictionary

a **un, una**
a lot **mucho/a**
above **arriba**
ache, the **dolor, el**
aeroplane, the **avión, el**
afterwards **después**
agreed **de acuerdo**
airport, the **aeropuerto, el**
alright **bien**
also **también**
always **siempre**
all **todo**
all right **vale**
American **americano/a**
and **y**
and so **entonces**
apartment, the **piso, el**
appointment, an **cita, una**
April **abril**
are **son**
aren't they? **¿verdad?**
as **como**
ask (to) **preguntar**
August **agosto**

bad **malo/a**
bag, the **bolsa, la**
Bank of Spain, the **Banco de España, el**
bathroom, the **cuarto de baño, el**
because **porque**
beer, the **cerveza, la**
behind **detrás (de)**

below **abajo**
better **mejor**
big **grande**
bill, the **cuenta, la**
black **negro/a**
blue **azul**
boat, the **barco, el**
book, the **libro, el**
boring **aburrido/a**
bottle, a **botella, una**
bread, the **pan, el**
breakfast, the **desayuno, el**
broken **roto/a**
broken down **rota/a**
brown **marrón**
bus, the **autobús, el**
but **pero**
butter, the **mantequilla, la**
buy (to) **comprar**
bye **hasta luego**

café, a **cafetería, una**
call (to call on the phone) **llamar (por teléfono)**
called, has **ha llamado**
Can I ask you? **¿Puedo preguntarle?**
car, the **coche, el**
carbonated/non-carbonated **con/sin gas**
cashpoint machine, a **cajero (automático), un**
cent **céntimo, el**

Christmas, at Christmas
   Navidad, en Navidad
clean **limpio/a**
client, the **cliente, el**
coffee **café**
cold **frío/a**
cold, a **resfriado, un**
colours, the **colores, los**
college, a **colegio, un**
come (to) **venir**
come!, come on! **¡venga!**
come off it! **¡qué va!**
company, the **empresa, la**
computers, the **ordenadores,
   los**
correct **correcto**
could you help me? **¿podría
   ayudarme?**
crazy **loco/a**
credit cards, the **tarjetas de
   crédito, las**
charming **amable**
cheap **barato/a**
cheese, the **queso, el**
chemist's, the **farmacia, la**
child, the (f) **hija, la**
child, the (m.) **hijo, el**
children, the **niños, los**
chips, the **patatas fritas, las**
chops, the **chuletas, las**
church, the **iglesia, la**

daughter, the **hija, la**
days of the week, the **días de
   la semana, los**
December **diciembre**
dessert, the **postre, el**
do (to) **hacer**
do you like? **¿le gusta?**
doctor, the **doctor, el**
dog, a **perro, un**

don't you? **¿verdad?**
door, the **puerta, la**
double room, a **habitación
   doble, una**
downstairs **abajo**
drink (to) **beber**
drink, a **copa, una**
dry cleaner's, the **tintorería,
   la**
during **durante**

easy **fácil**
eat (to) **comer**
eggs, the **huevos, los**
eight **ocho**
e-mail, the **correo
   electrónico, el**
end, the **final, el**
England **Inglaterra**
English **inglés**
enough **suficiente, bastante**
excuse me **perdón**
exit, the **salida, la**
expensive **caro/a**

February **febrero**
fillet steak, a **filete, un**
finished **terminado**
first **primero**
fish, the **pescado, el**
five **cinco**
flat, the **piso, el**
football, the **fútbol, el**
for **para, por, durante**
for me **para mí**
forbidden **prohibido**
four **cuatro**
Friday **viernes**
from **de/del**
from here to there **de acá
   para allá**

fruit, the **fruta, la**
full **lleno/a**

garlic, the **ajo, el**
girlfriend, a **amiga, una**
glass, a **vaso, un**
go (to) **ir**
good **bueno/a**
good afternoon **buenas tardes**
good day **buenos días**
good grief! (lit. my mother!) **¡Madre mía!**
good morning **buenos dias**
good night **buenas noches**
goodbye, for longer absence **adiós**
good looking **guapo/a**
gram, a **gramo, un**
great **estupendo/a**
green **verde**
grey **gris**

hairdresser's the **peluquería, la**
half **medio/a**
ham, the **jamón, el**
handbag, the **bolso, el**
he, him **él**
he/she/it can **puede**
he/she/it comes **viene**
he/she/it gives **da**
he/she/it goes **va**
he/she/it has **tiene**
he/she/it is **está**
he/she/it lives **vive**
he/she/it says **dice**
he/she/it smokes **fuma**
he/she/it speaks **habla**
he/she/it was **era**
he/she/it works **trabaja**

headache, the **dolor de cabeza, el**
hello **hola**
her **ella**
here **aquí**
him **él**
home, at **casa, en**
hospital, the **hospital, el**
hot **caliente**
house, a **casa, una**
how… ? **¿cómo… ?**
how are you? **¿qué tal?**
how does one say in Spanish… ? **¿cómo se dice en español… ?**
how is… ? **¿qué tal?**
how much… ? **¿cuánto?**
hundred, a **cien**
husband, the **marido, el**

I **yo**
I am **soy**
I am going **voy**
I believe **creo**
I can **puedo**
I do not like (it) **no me gusta**
I go **voy**
I have **tengo**
I have been, I was **he estado**
I have bought, I bought **he comprado**
I have gone **he ido**
I have seen **he visto**
I have to, must **tengo que**
I have worked **he trabajado**
I hope **espero**
I know (something) **sé**
I know (usually somebody or a place) **conozco (a)**
I like (it) **me gusta**
I see **veo**

I speak **hablo**
I understand **comprendo**
I was **era**
I work **trabajo**
I would like (to) **quisiera**
I'm sorry **lo siento**

ice cream, an **helado, un**
if **si**
ill **enfermo/a**
important **importante**
in/on **en**
in front of **delante (de)**
interesting **interesante**
isn't it? **¿verdad?**
it **lo, la**
it costs **cuesta**
it doesn't matter **no importa**
it is bad weather (lit. it makes…) **hace mal tiempo**
it is cold (it makes cold) **hace frío**
it is that… **es que…**

January **enero**
July **julio**
June **junio**

kilometre, the **kilómetro, el**
kind **amable**
know (to know a fact) **saber**

lamb, the **cordero, el**
last **último/a**
later **más tarde, luego**
less **menos**
let's go! **¡vamos!**
letter, the **carta, la**
letter box, the **buzón, el**
like **como**
litre, the **litro, el**

little, a little **poco, un poco**
lovely **bonito/a**

main road, the **carretera, la**
make (to) **hacer**
map, the **mapa, el**
march **marzo**
marvellous **estupendo/a**
matter, a **cosa, una**
May **mayo**
me **yo**
meat, the **carne, la**
menu, the **menú, el**
milk, the **leche, la**
minutes **minutos**
mobile (phone), the **(teléfono) móvil, el**
moment, a **momento, un**
Monday **lunes**
money, the **dinero, el**
months, the **meses, los**
more **más**
more slowly **más despacio**
mother, the **madre, la**
motor, the **motor, el**
motorway, the **autovía, la**
Mrs **señora**
much **mucho/a**
my **mi**
my name is… **me llamo**

name, the **nombre, el**
near **cerca**
never **nunca**
new **nuevo/a**
newspaper, a **periódico, un**
next week (the week that comes) **semana que viene, la**
nice **bonito/a**
night, a **noche, una**

nine **nueve**
no **no**
no problem **no importa**
nobody **nadie**
non-smoking **no fumadores**
not **no**
nothing **nada**
November **noviembre**
now **ahora**
numbers **números**

October **octubre**
of **de**
of the **de/del**
oil, the **aceite, el**
OK **de acuerdo, vale**
old **viejo/a**
on **en**
on holiday(s) **de vacaciones**
on the left **a la izquierda**
on the move **de acá para allá**
on the right **a la derecha**
on the telephone **por teléfono**
one **uno; un, una**
one cannot do that **no se
    puede hacer**
only **sólo**
open **abierto**
or **o**
orange **naranja**
other, the **otro, el/otra, la**
our **nuestro/a**

pain, the **dolor, el**
paper, the **papel, el**
pay, the **sueldo, el**
people, the **gente, la**
perhaps **quizás**
petrol, the **gasolina, la**
petrol station, the **gasolinera, la**
photo, the **foto, la**

pink **rosa**
platform, the **via, la**
please **por favor**
pleased **contento/a**
police, the **policia, la**
possible **posible**
post office, the **correos**
postcards, the **tarjetas, las**
pretty **bonito/a**
price, the **precio, el**
problem, the **problema, el**

quarter **cuarto**

railway, the **ferrocarril, el**
rain, the **lluvia, la**
rather **bastante**
red **rojo/a**
red wine, the **vino tinto, el**
repair (to) **reparar**
repair garage, the **taller, el**
restaurant, the **restaurante, el**
return ticket ('going and
    returning') **ida y vuelta**
river, the **río, el**
roast chicken, the **pollo
    asado, el**

said, has **ha dicho**
salad, a **ensalada, una**
salary, the **sueldo, el**
sales assistant, the
    dependiente, el
same, the **mismo, el**
Saturday **sábado**
say (to) **decir**
school, a **colegio, un**
seats, the **asientos, los**
second **segundo/a**
September **septiembre**
seven **siete**

she **ella**
ship, the **barco, el**
shoes, the **zapatos, los**
shop, the **tienda, la**
shopping, (to) go **ir de compras**
shower, the **ducha, la**
sick **enfermo/a**
since **desde**
six **seis**
size, the **talla, la**
slow **lento/a**
small **pequeño/a**
smoke (to) **fumar**
snobbish **esnob**
snow, the **nieve, la**
some **unos, unas**
someone **alguien**
something **algo**
son, the **hijo, el**
soup, a **sopa, una**
Spanish chain of department stores, a **Corte Inglés, El**
Spanish omelette, a **tortilla, una**
Spanish snacks **tapas**
speak **hable**
stamps, the **sellos, los**
station, the **estación, la**
stop, the **parada, la**
straight ahead **todo recto**
street, the **calle, la**
sugar, the **azúcar, el**
suitcase, a **maleta, una**
sun, the **sol, el**
Sunday **domingo**
supermarket, a **supermercado, un**
sure (about) **seguro (de)**

table, the **mesa, la**
take (to) **tomar**

tea, a **té, un**
ten **diez**
terrible **terrible**
thank you **gracias**
thank you very much **muchas gracias**
that **ese, esa/eso (by itself)**
that, as **que**
that's because… **es que…**
the **el, la, los, las**
then **después, luego**
there **allí**
there is **hay**
they are **están, son**
they come **vienen**
they cost **cuestan**
they do **hacen**
they say **dicen**
they were **eran**
thing, a **cosa, una**
thirty five **treinta y cinco**
thirty metres **treinta metros**
this **este, esta/esto (by itself)**
this one **éste**
three **tres**
Thursday **jueves**
ticket, the **billete, el**
time, the **tiempo, el**
to the centre **al centro**
to, to the **a/al**
toast **tostada**
tobacconist, the **estanco, el**
today **hoy**
toilets, the **servicios, los**
tomorrow **mañana**
too **demasiado**
too much **demasiado**
traffic light, the **semáforo, el**
train, the **tren, el**
T-shirt, the **camiseta, la**
Tuesday **martes**

TV, the **tele, televisión, la, la**
two **dos**

underground, the **metro, el**
unfortunately
  desgraciadamente
until **hasta**
until later **hasta luego**
upstairs **arriba**
us **nos**

vegetables, the **verdura, la**
very **muy**

wait (formal) **espere**
wait (friendly) **espera**
wait (to) **esperar**
waiter, the **camarero, el**
water, the **agua (f.), el**
we **nosotros**
we are **somos**
we are going **vamos**
we arrive **llegamos**
we can **podemos**
we do **hacemos**
we go **vamos**
we have **tenemos**
we have been, we were **hemos estado**
we have eaten **hemos comido**
we have to **tenemos que**
we know **conocemos**
we must **tenemos que**
we take **tomamos**
we work **trabajamos**
we would like (to)
  quisiéramos
we write **escribimos**
weather, the **tiempo, el**
Wednesday **miércoles**

well **bien**
well then **pues…**
well, hello! (surprise greeting)
  ¡hombre!
well… **pues…**
what? **¿qué?**
what a bore! **¡qué lata!**
what a nuisance! **¡qué lata!**
what do you have? **¿qué tienen ustedes?**
what do you want? **¿qué quiere?**
what do you wish? **¿qué desean?**
what is happening? **¿qué pasa?**
what is the matter? **¿qué pasa?**
when? **¿cuándo?**
where? **¿dónde?**
white **blanco/a**
who? **¿quién?**
why? **¿por qué?**
wife, the **mujer, la**
with **con**
without **sin**
woman, the **señora, mujer, la**
work, the **trabajo, el**
Would you mind? **¿Le importaría?**

year, the **año, el**
years, the **años, los**
yellow **amarillo/a**
yes **sí**
yesterday **ayer**
you (one person) **usted**
you (more than one person)
  ustedes
you are (singular), you are
  (plural) **estás, están**

110

you can **puedes**
you come **vienes**
you do **haces**
you give **das**
you go **vas**
you have **tienes**
you like **le gusta**

you live **vives**
you say **dices**
you smoke **fumas**
you speak **hablas**
you work **trabajas**

zero **cero**

How to use the flash cards

Learning words and sentences can be tedious but with flash cards it's quick and good fun.

This is what you do

When the **Day-by-day guide** tells you to use the cards cut them out, photocopy them or copy them on to card. There are 22 **Flash words** and 10 **Flash sentences** for each week. Each card has a little number on it telling you to which week it belongs, so you won't cut out too many cards at a time or muddle them up later on.

First try to learn the words and sentences by looking at both sides. Then, when you have a rough idea start testing yourself – that's the fun bit. Look at the English, say the Spanish, and then check. Make two piles: 'correct' and 'wrong' or 'don't know'. When all the cards are used up, start again with the 'wrong' pile and try to whittle it down until you get all of them right. You can also play it 'backwards' by starting with the Spanish face up.

Take them with you on the bus, the train, to the hairdresser's or the dentist. Do a quick 'turn and learn' whenever you have a bit of spare time

The 22 **Flash words** of each lesson are there to start you off. Convert the rest of the **New words** to **Flash cards**, too. It's well worth it!

> **Flash cards for 'fast' learning:**
> **Don't lose them – use them!**

1 **tenemos**	1 **¿qué tal?**
1 **vamos**	1 **voy**
1 **he estado**	1 **para**
1 **en casa**	1 **trabajo**
1 **he trabajado**	1 **ahora**
1 **estamos/ somos**	1 **tengo**

Cut out and use ✂

113

how are you? ₁	we have ₁
I go ₁	we go, we are going, let's go ₁
for ₁	I have been, I was ₁
I work ₁	at home ₁
now ₁	I have worked ₁
I have ₁	we are ₁

Cut out and use ✂

1 **tiene**	1 **siempre**
1 **está/es**	1 **también**
1 **de vacaciones**	1 **desgraciada-mente**
1 **con**	1 **cuesta/cuestan**
1 **el dinero**	1 **ahora**
2 **a la derecha**	2 **a la izquierda**

Cut out and use

always [1]	**he/she/it has, you have** [1]
also [1]	**he/she/it is, you are** [1]
unfortunately [1]	**on holiday** [1]
it costs, they cost [1]	**with** [1]
now [1]	**the money** [1]
on the left [2]	**on the right** [2]

Cut out and use ✂

2 **algo**	2 **caro/cara**
2 **cerca**	2 **comer**
2 **¿cuánto…?**	2 **¿dónde…?**
2 **el desayuno**	2 **estupendo/a**
2 **hay**	2 **ir**
2 **la cuenta**	2 **luego**

expensive 2	**something** 2
(to) eat 2	**near** 2
where...? 2	**how much...?** 2
great 2	**the breakfast** 2
(to) go 2	**there is, there are** 2
then, afterwards 2	**the bill** 2

Cut out and use ✂

2	2
muy	**puedo**

2	2
podemos	**quisiéramos**

2	2
menos	**el marido**

2	2
malo	**los servicios**

3	3
primero	**un cajero (automático)**

3	3
el estanco	**correos**

I can ²	**very** ²
we would like (to) ²	**we can** ²
the husband ²	**less** ²
the toilets ²	**bad** ²
a cash point machine ³	**first** ³
the post office ³	**the tobacconist's** ³

3	3
comprar	**los sellos**
3	3
después	**quizás**
3	3
quisiera	**tengo que**
3	3
hasta	**abierto/a**
3	3
más tarde	**los huevos**
3	3
bastante	**ayer**

Cut out and use ✂

3	3
the stamps	**(to) buy**
3	3
perhaps	**afterwards**
3	3
I have to, I must	**I would like (to)**
3	3
open	**until**
3	3
the eggs	**later**
3	3
yesterday	**enough**

 Cut out and use

3 **¿quién?**	3 **un periódico**
3 **la farmacia**	3 **la mantequilla**
3 **creo**	3 **nuevo**
4 **el agua**	4 **alguien**
4 **arriba**	4 **delante (de)**
4 **detrás (de)**	4 **el pescado**

Cut out and use ✂

3 **a newspaper**	3 **who?**
3 **the butter**	3 **the pharmacy**
3 **new**	3 **I believe**
4 **someone**	4 **the water**
4 **in front of**	4 **above, upstairs**
4 **the fish**	4 **behind**

Cut out and use ✂

4 **está bien**	4 **¿cómo?**
4 **la salida**	4 **me gusta**
4 **nadie**	4 **nuestro, nuestra**
4 **seguro**	4 **terminado**
4 **un resfriado**	4 **un vaso**
4 **una cosa**	4 **venir**

Cut out and use ✂

how? 4	it's all right 4
I like 4	the exit 4
our 4	nobody 4
finished 4	sure 4
a glass 4	a cold 4
(to) come 4	a thing, matter 4

Cut out and use ✂

4	4
conozco (a)	**beber**
4	4
un perro	**el dolor**
5	5
la estación	**venga**
5	5
la parada	**allí**
5	5
abajo	**el buzón**
5	5
hacer	**¿por qué?**

drink, to drink `4`	I know `4`
the pain `4`	a dog `4`
come, come on `5`	the station `5`
there `5`	the stop `5`
the letter box `5`	below, downstairs `5`
why? `5`	(to) make, do `5`

Cut out and use ✂

5	5
lleno	**el otro, la otra**

5	5
el coche	**la calle**

5	5
si	**la gasolina**

5	5
el taller	**caliente**

5	5
la lluvia	**contento/a**

5	5
el problema	**comprendo**

5 the other	5 full
5 the street	5 the car
5 the petrol	5 if
5 hot	5 the garage
5 pleased	5 the rain
5 I understand	5 the problem

Cut out and use

5	5
el billete	**¿cuándo?**
6	6
el aeropuerto	**esperar**
6	6
decir	**en Navidad**
6	6
la nieve	**¡qué lata!**
6	6
¡hombre!	**¿Le importaría?**
6	6
veo	**nunca**

Cut out and use ✂

when? 5	**the ticket** 5
(to) wait 6	**the airport** 6
at Christmas 6	**(to) say** 6
what a bore! 6	**the snow** 6
would you mind? 6	**well, hello!** 6
never 6	**I see** 6

Cut out and use

6 **¿qué pasa?**	6 **¡espere!**
6 **el piso**	6 **sé**
6 **saber**	6 **la gente**
6 **llamar (por teléfono)**	6 **conocemos**
6 **el libro**	6 **el barco**
6 **hacen**	6 **el año que viene**

6	6
wait!	**What is the matter?**
I know	**the flat, apartment**
the people	**(to) know**
we know	**to call (on the phone)**
the boat, ship	**the book**
next year	**they do, you do**

Cut out and use ✂

Vamos a Madrid. 1

He estado en Marbella. 1

para mi empresa 1

Tengo una casa. 1

Tenemos dos niños. 1

Voy a casa. 1

Trabajo en Londres. 1

He trabajado muchos años. 1

El trabajo es bueno. 1

¿Está de vacaciones? 1

Cut out and use ✂

We go/Let's go to Madrid. 1

I have been/I was in Marbella. 1

for my company 1

I have a house. 1

We have two children. 1

I go/am going home. 1

I work in London. 1

I worked/have worked many years. 1

The work is good. 1

Are you/Is he, she on holiday? 1

Cut out and use

¿Tiene usted una habitación? 2

¿Dónde está la cafetería? 2

¿Cuánto cuesta? 2

¿Hay un banco aquí? 2

Quisiéramos ir a Marbella. 2

a las diez y media 2

La cuenta, por favor. 2

Tengo una tarjeta de crédito. 2

No puedo ir. 2

¿A qué hora podemos comer? 2

Cut out and use ✂

137

Do you have a room? 2

Where is the café? 2

How much does it cost? 2

Is there a bank here? 2

We would like to go to Marbella. 2

at half past ten 2

The bill, please. 2

I have a credit card. 2

I cannot go. 2

At what time can we eat? 2

Cut out and use

Voy de compras. 3

Tengo que ir de compras. 3

Hace mal tiempo. 3

Lo siento. 3

He comprado demasiado. 3

No importa. 3

Quisiera comprar… 3

He ido al supermercado. 3

Tenemos que comprar… 3

¿Ha visto…? 3

Cut out and use

I am going shopping. 3

I must go shopping. 3

It is bad weather. 3

I am sorry. 3

I have bought too much. 3

It does not matter. 3

I would like to buy... 3

I have gone to the supermarket. 3

We have to buy... 3

Have you seen...? 3

Cut out and use

Alguien ha llamado. 4

No ha dicho para qué. 4

Es una cosa importante. 4

La semana que viene tenemos tiempo. 4

Eso es posible. 4

Me gusta mucho. 4

El ajo no me gusta. 4

¿Le gusta el hotel? 4

¿Podría ayudarme, por favor? 4

¿Cómo se dice… en español? 4

Cut out and use ✂

Someone has called. 4

He/She did not say why. 4

It is an important matter. 4

We have time next week. 4

That is possible. 4

I like it very much. 4

I do not like garlic. 4

Do you like the hotel? 4

Can you help me please? 4

How do you say… in Spanish? 4

Cut out and use ✂

dos billetes de ida y vuelta 5

Hable más despacio, 5
por favor.

¿Cuándo hay un tren? 5

Voy a hacer algo. 5

Estoy muy contento/a. 5

Esperamos que sí. 5

¿Dónde está la carretera? 5

¿Por qué lo compra? 5
¡Porque me gusta!

Hablo sólo un poco 5
español.

Si hay un coche, lo tomamos. 5

two return tickets 5

Please speak more slowly. 5

When is there a train? 5

I am going to do something. 5

I am very happy. 5

We hope so. 5

Where is the main road? 5

Why are you buying it? 5
Because I like it!

I only speak a little Spanish. 5

If there is a car we'll have it. 5

Cut out and use ✂

¿Qué tal sus vacaciones? 6

¿Le importaría ayudarme? 6

¿Le importaría darme…? 6

¿Qué pasa con…? 6

¡Vamos a tomar una copa! 6

No he ido nunca a Barcelona. 6

Tenemos que trabajar.
¡Qué lata! 6

He esperado durante una
semana. 6

¿Qué ha hecho? 6

Tienen un piso. Lo sé. 6

Cut out and use ✂

How are/were your holidays? 6

Would you mind helping me? 6

Would you mind giving me...? 6

What's the matter with...? 6

Let's go and have a drink! 6

I've never been to Barcelona. 6

We must work. What a bore! 6

I waited for a week. 6

What did you do? 6

They have a flat.
I know that. 6

Cut out and use ✂

This is to certify
that

. . . .

has successfully completed
a six-week course of

Fast Spanish
with Elisabeth Smith

with

. . . .

results

Date . . . .

Author *Elizabeth Smith*

Praise for Elisabeth Smith

'A language lifeline ... fun, fast and easy.'
(*The Independent*)

'The simple scripts and audio make it crystal clear ... I'm delighted with my progress.'
(*Greece* magazine)

'Its narration is laid-back and encouraging and the method is straightforward. (4-star review)'
(*Time Out*)

'The elements are simple and very straightforward ... strong encouragement ... plenty of opportunity for spoken practice. This course worked very well for me.'
(*Professional Manager* magazine)

'We think it is wonderful.'
(Tom and Maureen Peil, Preston)

'I loved the sense of humour ... Each week I did the final test with bated breath wondering if this time the little bar chart [...] would take a nose dive – but it didn't.'
(Lesly Hopkins, Twickenham)

'This isn't just a package that asks you remember the names for things in a different language this is a package that teaches ... Highly recommended.'
(Maximus)

'It really is an effective way to learn.'
(Mr R. Ellor)

'A solid product offering excellent value for money ... a great place to start.'
(A. M. Boughey)

'One of the best courses around to get you that little bit further than the basics.'
(Johannsen Krister)

more...

'The words are very clearly spoken and the form of presentation witty and lively to keep your interest, and clever choice of subject matter also keep learning interesting and aid memory. This is a very strong language course and I recommend it.'
(vh1967)

'The Elisabeth Smith courses are a superb resource for the learner who needs to be able to speak the language in a short period of time and with a good degree of understanding.'
(Will Boyce)

'I was surprised at what I'd achieved after this course and recommend it.'

'This is an absolute must have ... You'll be so glad you bought it!'
(Elodie)

Now join me on:

Facebook at www.facebook.com/elisabethsmithlanguages

Twitter at www.twitter.com/LanguagesESmith